JOHN DEWEY *in perspective*

JOHN DEWEY

in perspective

GEORGE R. GEIGER

New York
Oxford University Press
1958

Library of Congress Catalogue Card Number 58–9463

Printed in the United States of America

Preface

THE approach of John Dewey's centennial year in 1959 will undoubtedly stimulate a renewed interest in the life and work of America's most influential and controversial thinker. It should also begin to make possible a sense of perspective and of summary, which has not always been present in the discussion of his ideas. Too often the limited focus of such discussion has tended to obscure the spacious outlines of his philosophic picture. In the present work the misconceptions, the stereotypes, the criticisms will be examined in the light of Deweys' own writings. And to correct the sometimes narrow and occasionally vulgar interpretation of his philosophy there will be deliberate emphasis on the consummatory and esthetic aspects of Dewey's philosophy of experience.

Anyone who writes about Dewey must acknowledge his indebtedness to the many commentaries already available, chiefly those of Sidney Hook, and also of Joseph Ratner, Jerome Nathanson, Ernest Nagel, Irwin Edman, and many others. But the range of Dewey's achievement is so wide that still another interpretation, admittedly personal and incomplete, may help to contribute to the centennial appraisal of a dominating intellectual figure.

Preface

I want to thank the Oxford University Press for having suggested the book in the first place, and Elizabeth Cameron for helping to remove many errors of interpretation and expression. The errors that may remain are not her fault. The publishers of the books mentioned in the bibliography and footnotes must be thanked for their kind permission to quote from Dewey's writings.

G. R. G.

Antioch College
Yellow Springs, Ohio
June, 1958

Contents

JOHN DEWEY *in perspective*

1. The Affirmation of Experience

This is a peculiar time in which to be writing about John Dewey. It is a time when almost every fundamental part of his philosophy seems to have been rejected. Are we not now being reminded that man is indeed a fallen creature whose original sin is pride, pride in his intelligence? Not knowing this, he has been living in a dusty wasteland. Or perhaps we are told—for some time now and from sources equally respectable—that man is a stranger here who cannot, within himself, find meaning or hope in his bizarre existence. As the emphasis shifts a little, we are advised with much solemnity that scientific inquiry is morally neutral and can afford no help in social or political affairs, that what we need is good will alone and faith in a supreme source of value. This, we learn, is our only weapon against communism. Piety becomes a political virtue as a new conservatism takes on style. The intellectuals flirt with mysticism while the general public devours inspirational books and the news magazines report the details of fashionable conversions. Education is to go back to the eternal verities.

These observations frankly are impressionistic. Which is to say accurate, even if fragmentary. And although each of them can be documented, it might be rash to keep repeating that we are in hot 'retreat from reason' as the 'new failure of nerve' spreads from poetry to religion and now to politics. To categorize an age, especially a present one, is risky; it is still more so to predict its duration. There may even be some small evidence that our 'age of anxiety' has itself become a tiresome cliché about to be replaced by another: 'the age of conformity,' or 'the age of indifference.' We cannot be flippant about it. There undoubtedly is good reason for men to be scared and disillusioned, although it may be urged that such good reason be sought in the social scene rather than in that of private and 'existentialist' malaise. Dewey himself was quite aware that many men had lost their nerve. As a matter of fact, if he had not been, something would have been wrong with his own idea that philosophy is in great part a reflex of current cultural conflicts.

This, then, is a necessary time to write about Dewey. It is a time when almost every fundamental part of his philosophy seems also to have been misperceived; vulgarization and stereotyping have just about taken over. Again, there is nothing unique or surprising about this. The product of every original and provocative thinker is inevitably going to be simplified, oversimplified, and ultimately distorted; and it is a nice question how the responsibility for the distortion should be allocated. If contemporary Marxism as professed, say, in the Soviet Union is not what 'Marx really meant'; if Freud is unfairly represented by certain extravagant misapplications of his ideas; if notions of the contributions of Darwin, Einstein, or even Thomas Aquinas are more prevalent than accurate, who is to blame? Emerson warned, 'Beware when the great God lets loose a thinker on this planet,' and one reason for his warning would seem to be that the ideas of the thinker are vigorous and challenging enough to be appropriated, or condemned, by many men. If this must mean misappropriation, with the ideas being tied to interpretations the thinker would surely have repudiated, that is still no more than testimony to his influence and the magic of his presence.

Be that as it may, it cannot be denied that the perceptions —or misperceptions—people have of a maker of ideas bear weight and must be reckoned with. 'Deweyism' is an American stereotype. Much of what passes under that title has little to do with the philosophy of a man called John Dewey; but nevertheless it cannot be ignored. (It is unnecessary to add that a stereotype can be 'for' as well as 'against.' Nor is it necessary to point out that stereotyping is a natural process and that without its economy communication would be restricted almost to the point of uselessness. We may recognize that Frenchman_1 is not Frenchman_2, yet if we could not use a 'French' stereotype to contrast, for instance, with a 'German' one, we would indeed be hampered in our discourse.)

It is, of course, in the field of education that the Dewey myth is most apparent. When his name is not used, then 'progressive' acts as a surrogate. In recent years, the connotations clustering around this term have been largely negative, but not entirely so. Dewey's influence in education is seen as something like this (and almost every phrase used is itself hardly more than a slogan): 'learning by doing'; 'projects'; 'the child-centered school'; 'interest and effort'; 'permissiveness.' In short, the romantic cult of the child. These soon are transformed into: 'lack of discipline'; 'illiteracy'; 'anarchy'; 'anti-intellectualism'; 'barbarism.' (I am quoting.) From another sector of the educational front the view might be: 'social studies'; 'radical'; 'subversive'; 'un-American'; and 'atheistic.' Then there is a special category—teachers colleges (usually followed by an exclamation mark). To be sure, these ideas may also be phrased positively: 'intrinsic interest in the child'; 'individual development'; 'critical thinking'; 'growth'; 'democracy.' It should be added, in the interest of fairness, that recently some of the more responsible critics are acknowledging publicly that what they are attacking is not necessarily to be attributed to John Dewey. Still he serves as whipping-boy, bogeyman, and salve.

Next there are the clichés connected with 'pragmatism': 'truth is what works'; 'a vulgar businessman's philosophy, typically American' (this is usually a transatlantic misperception); 'a philosophy of capitalist imperialism' (a communist contribution). More sophisticated labels read: 'materialism'; 'moral relativity' and 'nihilism'; 'cosmic impiety'; 'an exaggerated humanism leading eventually to subjectivism and idealism.' And the spectrum is complete from infra-red to ultra-violet. When a dominating thinker is perceived as both materialist and idealist, as bourgeois imperialist and atheistic communist, relativist and dogmatist, do-gooder and crypto-fascist (and there is ample documentation for each), we not only see that these views tend to cancel each other but begin to ask if there is indeed a common focus at which they are directed.

If, then, we try to describe the reconstruction that Dewey sought to accomplish and to trace some of the effects of that reconstruction, the chief problem is to decide upon a common focus. Because Dewey's views on education and society are most familiar and have also produced some of the more egregious misinterpretations, it might seem plausible to consider these views first. As strong a case could be made for giving priority to other interests such as logic and theory of knowledge. The fact is that every subject-matter Dewey considers is in a sense illustrative of an overarching point of view. While there may be no classical system in the grand style to be found in his works, there is certainly a unifying theme that runs through all the material he handles. That theme has many variations, all of them part of a long, discriminating celebration of experience.

For most of us, 'experience' is probably one of many undefined terms, something unanalyzed, taken for granted, about which we seem to know a great deal until we are questioned about it. If we are pressed, then 'experience' becomes that which is direct and immediate rather than vicarious or second-hand, as when we say we underwent an accident and did not merely read about it in the papers, or when we talk of learning by experience instead of from books. It can also refer to something noteworthy and compelling—'*that* was an experience!' Pressed still further, we may finally locate experience in the dimension of a private consciousness cut off from nature and the world, a kind of comment on reality. Regarded now as something subjective and exclusively mental, it is split off from the objective state of affairs. The phrase 'nature and experience' is likely to become the sign not only of a split but of an antithesis, the word 'and' changing into 'versus.'

Such a separation of experience from the 'outside' physical world would not be merely a popular conceit. It has a respectable lineage in philosophy, stretching back to the antique Greek dualisms, and in modern thought is reinforced even by those who have been pleased to call themselves empiricists. The classic separation of appearance from reality keeps cropping up as the problem of knowledge or as the equally insoluble relation of mind to body; but the assumed discontinuity remains. Experience is somehow cut off, unnatural, not entirely trustworthy; it becomes an anomaly, a kind of general predicament. From here only a short step leads to its depreciation. This is so even when another step, in an entirely different direction, leads to a sentimental extension of the predicament so that experience is seen finally as encircling the world in one idealistic stride. Both these steps lead down paths that carry many away from the things of ordinary experience, which are in some sense unreal.

The tendency to discredit concrete human experience, even in its very description, has not been confined, Dewey feels, to professional philosophy but goes far beyond technical concerns such as theories of knowledge or mind-body problems. This discrediting is not mitigated—indeed it is established—by the exaggerated subjectivizing of what passes popularly for experience; and this, for Dewey, is a most serious matter. It means a turning away from that 'intellectual piety toward experience which is a precondition of the direction of life and of tolerant and generous cooperation among men. Respect for the things of experience alone brings with it such a respect for others, the centres of experience, as is free from patronage, domination, and the will to impose.'*

This should give the flavor of what is nothing less than a 'moral' or even a 'democratic' approach to experience. Experience is—or, rather, might be and should be—precious, consummated, and whole. Why is it otherwise? Why does experience first fall apart into fragments and end by being

* Dewey, John, *Experience and Nature,* Chicago, 1925, p. 36, quoted in Joseph Ratner's *The Philosophy of John Dewey*, Henry Holt, New York, 1928, p. 18.

explained away as something of an illusion? To answer this is not easy, because, for one thing, the fractures within experience seem so obvious that they ordinarily do not call for analysis or even definition: mind-body, subject-object, individual-social, ends-means, to go no further, appear to be pre-established dualities, between which interactions may occur but only in the sense of joining together precariously what already has been put asunder. Traditional philosophy and psychology have conspired to present human behavior as an uneasy fusion of originally separate entities. Now one, now another of these elements might be singled out for special attention, but such attention only reinforces their separateness. But it is not really philosophy or psychology which is involved here, for the inventory of dualism has been so built into our culture, into our very language, that it is all but impossible to think of experience except as a synthetic joining of paired opposites.

One 'explanation' for the obviousness and indefinability of these familiar splits within experience is simply that they are evident and intrinsic facts of existence. This is the way things are; and language, culture, and philosophy have only recognized what is indeed impossible not to recognize. However, another whole dimension of explanation—which is Dewey's—will suggest that there is nothing intrinsic or a priori about these alleged dualisms. If they seem incontrovertibly established, it may be that 'experience' itself has been culturally preconditioned and stereotyped for us.

The major thesis here is that philosophy, like science, religion, and the arts, is part of human culture, sharing its tensions and its inescapable distortions. This social thesis is basic for all of Dewey's work. Especially in the present context—that of trying to understand why man seems to have been living in two contrasting worlds—does an appeal to some primitive, massive social force appear indicated. In no other way, Dewey feels, can the cleavage in human culture be accounted for, that longtime cleavage between 'reality and appearance.' He asks us, therefore, to consider the perennial condition of insecurity, of a fundamental cosmic insecurity that did not have to wait for an Age of Anxiety to give it a loud voice. Man has always found himself coming up against a world dark, uncertain, fraught with peril and mystery, a forbidding and unintelligible world that demanded propitiation. True, it could be manipulated to a degree, but the realm of the practical and manipulative arts, of overt activity could never quite guarantee results. Seeds did not always sprout nor did the animal certainly fall in the hunt. Tools were refractory and the senses never entirely trustworthy. The problems of artisan or craftsman were often too much for him.

That early man compensated with myth and ceremony for these inadequacies in his control over nature is the theme of much of anthropology. What perhaps has not been so evident is that when metaphysics (or at least protometaphysics) did appear on the human scene, it proved to be a device that would contribute order and a rationale to the imaginative beliefs and practices of early man. These beliefs and practices were directed in great part to helping correct the imperfections of this world by celebrating another.

That other world, of course, would be a secure and reliable one, a happy hunting ground where no arrow missed its mark. To come into contact with such an absolutely trustworthy world—the world of real Reality—a special technique was necessary, just as special ceremonial techniques of dance and drama were necessary for other forms of communion. This special technique would be a way of knowing that was sure, universal, and revelatory, quite different from the fumbling way of the senses used by artisan and eoscientist, who were involved only in a world of 'mere' fact, of imperfection and uncertainty, in short, one of appearance. The man who really knew, call him priest, philosopher, or something else, was in direct touch with authentic reality, and his method of knowing it was superfine and extraordinary.

Even this fragmentary sketch of what Dewey has called 'the quest for certainty,' and which he has developed in detail throughout a number of books, should suggest a possible psycho-social source for the classic dualistic syndrome. The Christian religion and the official systems of European metaphysics, both based on the Greek notion of the two worlds of reality and appearance, of form and matter, look like a sophisticated and rationalized version of the need for a compensatory heaven of absolute goods. The need is as contemporary as it is ancient. For example, one reason why the Scientific Revolution of the sixteenth and seventeenth centuries failed to make decisive moral impact was that it developed in a cultural setting already dominated by the concept of intrinsic value, the value of repose in the finality of the 'real world.' Both philosophy and theology had conspired to keep alive a dichotomy going back to man's first bewildered response to what he saw around him, thus confronting the Scientific Revolution with a desperate counter-revolution, one which flourishes today as never before. Equally flourishing is that sense of insecurity which did not end with primitive man.

Dewey was hardly the first to advance an argument like

this. It was hinted at as early as the days of the Greek Sophists and was suggested by the Greek historians themselves; and since then it has become a familiar item in cultural history and social theory. Dewey did not invent the problem set up by the resistance developed by traditional beliefs to the forces of experimental knowledge, the resistance of folklore to science; although sometimes it seems as if he is held personally responsible for having put the new wine into the old bottles.

It is true that he was in a good position to notice the ferment and record the explosion. Dewey was born in 1859, the year Darwin's *On the Origin of Species* appeared—as a matter of fact it was published within five weeks of his birth. This in itself is a casual coincidence; but far from casual is the fact that Dewey lived for almost ninety-three years (and lived actively up to just about the very end), a period when Darwin's theories had their strongest impact. Dewey had a long view of the rise of new sciences and technologies and of their collision with the mores of a pre-evolutionary and pre-naturalistic culture. That Dewey accepted evolution suggests at least that he accepted biological continuity, which includes, among other things, the belief that live creatures are not divided from their environment in some irrecoverable fashion; that conscious experience and nature are not antithetical; that knowledge, therefore, is a matter of vital participation in a world of which it is a part rather than a matter of an outsider's disinterested glances.

To accept evolution means also to employ as a technique of analysis the historical and genetic method. This is what Dewey was doing when he tried to discover the sources of the familiar splitting of experience and suggested that they might be traced to man's earliest reactions to his surroundings and the subsequent freezing of these responses in social institutions. This kind of historical examination has oriented his entire philosophy. Although Dewey never wrote a major work on the history of philosophy, whatever he examined—esthetics, logic, metaphysics, and the rest—was examined, at least by way of introduction and setting, from an historical angle. Behind this interest was, of course, the evolutionary assumption that philosophical problems had a natural history; the particular argument here has been that the classic dualism between reality and appearance has also had a natural history. This, however, is not to say that the problem is nothing but its history.

But can 'experience' have a different meaning? Perhaps it is time to let Dewey speak for himself.

I begin with experience as the manifestation of interactions of organism and environment . . . Experience is not a veil that shuts man off from nature; it is a means of penetrating continually further into the heart of nature . . . Experience as an existence is something that occurs only under highly specialized conditions, such as are found in a highly organized creature which in turn requires a specialized environment. There is no evidence that experience occurs everywhere and everywhen. But candid regard for scientific inquiry also compels the recognition that when experience does occur, no matter at what limited portion of time and space, it enters into possession of some portion of nature and in such a manner as to render others of its precincts accessible . . . Experience is *of* as well as *in* nature. It is not experience which is experienced, but nature . . . Things interacting in certain ways *are* experience.*

* The first sentence is from *The Philosophy of John Dewey,* Schilpp, ed., The Library of Living Philosophers, Vol. I, Northwestern University,

That esthetic and moral experience reveals traits of real things as truly as does intellectual experience, that poetry may have a metaphysical import as well as science, is rarely affirmed, and when it is asserted, the statement is likely to be meant in some mystical or esoteric sense rather than in a straightforward everyday sense. Suppose however that we start with no presuppositions save that what is experienced, since it is a manifestation of nature, may, and indeed, must be used as testimony of the characteristics of natural events. Upon this basis, reverie and desire are pertinent for a philosophic theory of the true nature of things . . . The features of objects reached by scientific or reflective experience are important, but so are all the phenomena of magic, myth, politics, painting and penitentiaries. . . . The assumption of 'intellectualism' goes contrary to the facts of what is primarily experienced. For things are objects to be treated, used, acted upon and with, enjoyed and endured, even more than things to be known. They are things *had* before they are things cognized. (7: 19–21) *

Several questions may be raised at this point, questions raised, as a matter of fact, by Dewey himself. For one thing, is not this notion of experience as constituting the entire field of man's relation to the universe so broad as to be use-

---

Evanston, 1939, p. 531. The rest of the quotation is from *Experience and Nature*, Preface, iii, and pp. 3a, 4a. The edition used here, and which will be used from now on, is the second edition, 1929, in which the first chapter was rewritten making the pagination different from that of the 1925 edition.

References to Dewey's works are keyed to the bibliography found on page 237–8. The first number given will be that of the title as found in the bibliography and the second number or numbers will refer to the appropriate pages.

* It is of *Experience and Nature* that Justice Holmes said: 'If reduced to not more than two pages, it would be the profoundest aperçu of the universe that I have ever read."

less? Since the term includes literally everything man has dealings with, could it not simply be dropped? Dewey meets this question by suggesting that there is something indispensable about the term, 'namely an actual focusing of the world at one point . . . of immediate shining apparency'; and furthermore that 'reference to "experience" seems at present to be the easiest way of realizing the continuities among subject matters that are always getting split up into dualisms.' (4: 7, 71) In *Experience and Nature* he adds: 'we need a cautionary and directive word, like "experience," to remind us that the world which is lived, suffered and enjoyed as well as logically thought of, has the last word in all human inquiries and surmises.'* He is urging, then, that experience serve as a prophylactic against discontinuity, that it be employed to correct the partial empiricism which selects some aspects of experience as real and others as less so. This is why, at least at the time of writing *Experience and Nature,* Dewey was not prepared to give up the most generous use of 'experience,' even at the risk of imprecision.

However, he finally grew weary of defending it and in a paper written in his ninetieth year he admitted that the word could no longer be rescued from misinterpretation. The same point was made in what was his last book. In this work (*Knowing and the Known,* with Arthur F. Bentley), Dewey raised the vital question whether nontechnical words can be used fruitfully in philosophical discourse. Unlike Whitehead, who developed a new vocabulary to express his ideas, or at least changed radically the ordinary use of words to fit his needs, Dewey, at least until his final

* Ratner, op. cit. p. 15.

years, tried to confine himself to everyday language. This attempt proved a major contribution to misunderstanding, for when he uses relatively familiar labels such as 'practical,' 'idea,' 'problematic,' 'instrumental,' and many others, there is little chance that redefinition or extension of meaning will really take hold. 'Experience' is one of these labels.

In any event, whether 'experience' is employed or something possibly more felicitous, what should be emphasized is that the connotations called up by the term need to suggest continuity, process, situation, event, context—in short, 'transaction' rather than 'interaction.' This is not a matter of word-magic or of semantics. 'Transaction' became a key symbol in Dewey's final work because it calls up connection rather than disconnection, wholes rather than parts, continuity instead of discontinuity. A term like 'interaction,' on the other hand, already has begged the question of continuity, for it assumes that some things have indeed been set apart, the problem now being to put them together again. 'Transaction' implies a different kind of prejudgment, to the effect that there are units which can of course be broken apart for purposes of analysis but not for any other reason. For example, economic analysis may require that the processes of buying and selling be discussed separately. Yet the results of that analysis are not then read back into the buying-selling relationship, which is a transaction. To do so would be to sever them decisively, thereby making subsequent commerce between them problematic if not indeed mysterious. The origin of 'transaction' as a term lies unquestionably in the field of relations like buying-selling, lending-borrowing, and so on, but it is an appropriate symbol for a host of similarly unruptured relationships. Parent-child, husband-wife, cause-effect, end-means, would be illustrations. In all of these contexts one of the paired terms has no meaning without the other. True enough, the various transactions indicated do not necessarily exhaust the range of meaning of any one of the correlates: buyers are also sellers and, at other times, commercially disinterested; parents are not only and always parents; ends are themselves means. All this is obvious enough, yet it needs to be set down lest transactions be mistakenly regarded as something omnivorous, especially when we turn to another area of illustration.

However, within the various transactional situations, the related aspects are indeed mutual and completely interdependent, as they are in any 'field.' (Incidentally, Dewey's use of this now familiar term goes back to his earliest writings and may well antedate the general application of the word in physical theory.) Psychosomatic medicine; the gestalt concept in psychology, where the field or pattern is clearly a transaction between viewer and viewed; group theories in the social sciences; not to mention the field of force interpretation in physics—all would be additional illustrations of the transaction and of the idea that divisions within a given situation, when they are not arbitrary, are for specific analytical purposes of model making: the divisions are not necessarily intrinsic, original, or in the nature of things.

Experience, for Dewey, is a transaction. It is the name given to all that passes between the organism and its surroundings. Indeed, to be an organism is to be engaged in a transaction, which can be a limited one, as with the most simple forms of organic behavior, or the rich and enormously complicated activity of the self-conscious human being. In either case the transaction is a genuinely additive one, not a factitious or idle replica. It is additive because the organism is part of the natural world, not an intruder. Experience is a special kind of existence, just as real and special as the organism involved and no more outside nature than is the organism. It is the relation of part to whole, but the part *is* part of the whole. It would be tautologous, then, to point out that man cannot transcend his experience, since experience is binary, not solitary. A traveler cannot visit the places to which he does not travel. (Even Santayana, the realist, has noticed that 'our perceptions cannot tell us how the world would look if nobody saw it.') The waves a swimmer makes are authentic additions to the surface of the sea. To add that there are places where travelers do not go and that the sea is not profoundly affected by the swimmer does not change the observations.

It will be seen then that 'experience' stands for all commerce between man and nature—the gross, the physical, and the automatic as well as the refined and self-conscious. But all experience is not equally valuable. Dewey is not counseling a kind of indiscriminate wallowing. What gives significance to experience is that it be full and consummatory. On this point he writes:

> Oftentimes . . . things are experienced but not in such a way that they are composed into *an* experience. There is distraction and dispersion; what we observe and what we think, what we desire and what we get, are at odds with each other. We put our hands to the plow and turn back; we start and then we stop, not because the experience has reached the end for the sake of which it was initiated but because of extraneous interruptions or of inner lethargy.
>
> In contrast with such experience, we have *an* experience when the material experienced runs its course to fulfillment.

Then and then only is it integrated within and demarcated in the general stream of experience from other experiences . . . The esthetic is no intruder in experience from without . . . It is the clarified and intensified development of traits that belong to every normally complete experience. (11:35, 46.)

In short, experience is a natural phenomenon, a relationship between one part of existence and another. The relationship is a transactional one and truly relates: its effect is not to divide irretrievably one part of existence from another. It is an occasion for continuity, not the reverse. Experience, therefore, is neither opaque nor, to change the figure, omnivorous: it is not a barrier between man and nature nor does it swallow up the world. And although it may be in great part casual and even trivial or blind, experience contains within it the incandescence which will illuminate everything man is to prize. This is why 'experience' is the very signature of Dewey's philosophy. And this is why it makes a difference whether a full or narrow use of the term becomes dominant. For, as pointed out earlier, Dewey's purpose is essentially a moral one. He is attacking the notion that there is a private access to truth; that some portions of experience are intrinsically more privileged than others; and, above all, that there is something inauthentic about desiring, appreciating, and evaluating experiences.

It will be appropriate to see what Dewey means by a truly consummated experience, the kind we can call esthetic. For nowhere else is the empirical continuum he celebrates so vivid as here. 'The esthetic,' to repeat, 'is no intruder in experience from without . . . It is the clarified and intensified development of traits that belong to every normally complete experience.' To which he can add: '... Art—the mode of activity that is charged with meanings capable of immediately enjoyed possession—is the complete culmination of nature, and ... "science" is properly a handmaiden that conducts natural events to this happy issue.' (7:358)

This, then, is the central theme in all Dewey's thinking, the reverence—'piety,' it will be recalled, is the word he uses—for the total possibilities of human experience. His educational, social, scientific, and logical contributions, technical as they can become, are all geared to this end. It may prove to be a goal not easy to talk about, since the culminations of experience are matters of direct appreciation rather than of discourse, but to start here is, in any event, to start with what Dewey considers most important. It is also to start with some of his earliest writings, in which great pains were taken to show that experience is an affair of 'having' as well as of 'knowing.' Not that these are separate dimensions of experience, any more than ends are forever cut off from means; but, like ends and means, they can be handled separately. Ordinarily, discussion of Dewey's 'pragmatism' is limited to its problem-solving, instrumentalist aspects; those of thinking, knowing, scientific method, educational reform, and the like. But, while these are crucial, they are only 'handmaidens.' What they serve is 'art,' the memorializing of what life might become. It is to this side of Dewey that we turn, perhaps as prophylaxis against the infectious notion that his is a typically American philosophy, and therefore vulgar and short-sighted.

2. Experience as Art

The transaction that constitutes experience is a rhythmic affair. It is an affair of alternations, a movement—as William James put it—between 'perchings and flights,' an ebb and flow. Among the rhythms, for there are a number of them, is the oscillation between what we have and what we want, between enjoyment and the engineering of enjoyment, between the direct and the indirect, the 'having' and the 'knowing.' Dewey provides in various places a number of examples. Water in the context of satisfying thirst and water as the object of search or of analysis present two different kinds of experience. So does a fire when we poke it simply to enjoy the sparks or when we are trying to get the wood to burn by removing the ash. Or again, there is after-dinner conversation between friends in which the words become as autonomous and satisfying as the cigars and brandy, and there is talk to explain something or to make a political conversion.

Although different, these are not, of course, separate gears of experience between which we have to shift with some effort and noise. They can replace each other subtly and quickly, and sometimes, as when we poke the fire, it would be difficult to determine in precisely which gear we are moving. 'Knowing,' intellectual activity when it is not a chore or dull routine, partakes to some degree in the consummatory and final: the words we use to describe may themselves become enjoyed for their own sake. Indeed, Dewey feels that intellectual experience 'must bear an esthetic stamp to be itself complete.' Contrariwise, 'havings' and enjoyments are not necessarily final in the sense of being irresponsible and unforeseeing. Culminations are also beginnings. Authentic experience carries on; it is intervening as well as final, fruitful in that it leads to other genuine experiences. If not, there is the risk of dilettantism or even of the pathological, as when a situation of horror becomes so exquisite that action and redress give over to hypnotic fascination. But no single aspect of experience is exhaustive, since experience is not all of a piece; it is serial, 'an affair of histories,' as Dewey puts it.

The rhythms found in experience are not unique in the sense that they are exclusively a human affair. As experience is a transaction, it cannot be unilateral. The organism is acted upon and intersected by its surroundings as, in turn, it impresses itself on whatever it touches. Indeed, it is a nice problem to determine the precise contributions each element makes to the transaction, since 'the epidermis is only in the most superficial way an indication of where an organism ends and its environment begins.' (Arthur Bentley has called the human skin 'philosophy's last line of defense.') In any event, 'the live creature' is alive only because it is in direct contact with a world of moving, rhythmic energies, 'a world which is an impressive and irresistible mixture of sufficiencies, tight completenesses, order, recurrences which make possible prediction and control; and singularities, ambiguities, uncertain possibilities, processes going on to consequences as yet indeterminate.' It is a world of genuine hazard, contingency, and irregularity just as it is one of consummation, determinateness, and order. The matrix in which experience develops seems to be itself a temporal process of events, events which start and stop.

Almost any example would serve to disclose the pulsation constituting both organic and inorganic continuity. The cycles of the days and of the seasons, of waking and sleeping, of the crops and of life and death themselves; the ebb and flow of the waters and the moon and the blood; the very rhythm we proceed to call atom or even curve and number —these could be extended to include almost a definition of nature.

In this kind of correlation between the rhythms of experience and those of nature, it will be evident that Dewey advances an important argument, namely, that an analysis of experience is a trustworthy clue to traits of the world. Of course, such an argument has been implicit in the whole interpretation of experience-as-transaction, since, although only part of existence, experience is at least that part. Did it not afford genuine hints about what existence is like, one wonders how there could be a live creature at all. If human experience does partake of the character of the world of which it is a part, then the lineaments of authentic experience, of experience *in excelsis,* must also be traced to the controlling affinities between the live creature and its surroundings.

In a notable chapter of *Art as Experience,* 'The Natural History of Form,' Dewey endeavors to show the specific connections between the natural rhythms and tensions and the forms that help to determine the very definition of the arts. His thesis is clearly stated: 'Interaction of environment with organism is the source, direct or indirect, of all experience and from the environment come those checks, resistances, furtherances, equilibria, which, when they meet with the energies of the organism in appropriate ways, constitute form . . . Were it not so, rhythm as an essential property of form would be merely superimposed upon material, not an operation through which material effects its own culmination in experience . . . Form is arrived at whenever a stable, even though moving, equilibrium is reached.' (11:147, 14) This may seem a plausible interpretation, yet it has met serious criticism from, as it were, both the right and the left. For some it seems somehow vulgar and irrelevant, not to say downright degrading, since it supposedly 'reduces' the high affairs of esthetics to what man shares with the rest of nature. On the other hand, the imputing of feeling, even in embryo, to the inorganic world seems but an illustration of what Ruskin called 'the pathetic fallacy.' For example: 'Nature is kind and hateful, bland and morose, irritating and comforting, long before she is mathematically qualified or even a congeries of "secondary" qualities like colors and their shapes . . . *Things* are beautiful and ugly, lovely and hateful, dull and illuminated, attractive and repulsive. Stir and thrill in us is as much theirs as length, breadth, and thickness . . . Empirically, things are poignant, tragic, beautiful, humorous, settled, disturbed, comfortable, annoying, barren, harsh, consoling, splendid, fearful; are such immediately and in their own right and behalf.' (11:16; 7:108, 96.) When Dewey proceeds in this unbuttoned way, he seems like a Wordsworthian poet, even though the stereotypes topple. What he is doing is to turn in the opposite direction from that of the pathetic fallacy. Instead of reading qualities into nature he is, in a quite nonexistentialist fashion, deriving them from nature. As always, he is insisting on the recognition of continuity, in this case recognition of the naturalistic continuity which does not allow the live creature to fall out of its surroundings.

At this point, however, we must ask the question: What are the qualities of experience in its integrity and how are they implicit in the natural continuum of which all experience is a part? Or, in Dewey's formulation, we need to ask: What is *an* experience? When we say, '*That* meal, that storm, that rupture of friendship' was a *real* experience, what do we have in mind? Well, we certainly seem to intend that it is a unity. It hangs together, it is integrated and pervaded with a single dominating quality. It stands out by itself as a whole, as an organized pattern, clearly distinguished from anything else. It is indeed *an* experience and not merely a chaos of strung-along impressions. But why? Why do some items of memory or present consciousness carry with them their own self-sufficient individuality?

For one thing, it would appear that an experience, in its distinctive sense, is that which has come to a conclusion, not simply to an arbitrary stopping place. It has achieved a culmination, a fulfillment, and in this it is different from what, unfortunately, happens so often, which is that 'We put our hands to the plow and turn back; we start and then we stop, not because the experience has reached the end for the sake of which it was initiated but because of extraneous interruptions or of inner lethargy.' (11:35) But then there are the times when the game is played through, the problem satisfactorily closed, the spontaneous arrest of our attention transformed into a full, illuminating dénouement. There is resistance overcome, tension not simply released but fused into a new equilibrium; there is a sense of resolution and realization.

Such a feeling of completion is, Dewey believes, in harmony with natural rhythms. (Indeed, it may be argued that the equilibrium laws are the very key to all physical change.) 'Form' appears when such equilibrium is achieved, when some kind of enduring coherence develops out of interacting energies; and we speak without metaphor when we refer to the 'pattern' of an atom or a molecule, of a crystal or a nebula. True, the organic equilibria—the whole phenomenon of 'homeostasis'—are so much more conspicuous that they have tended to obscure the balances of the physical world; yet, although less intense, there is in the inorganic the same rhythm of break and recovery, of stopping and starting, of resistance overcome and energies redistributed for a new beginning. When this cycle not only persists in man but becomes conscious, 'it bears within itself the germs of a consummation akin to the esthetic.' (11:15)

There is nothing surprising about all this. After all, 'the nature of experience is determined by the essential conditions of life' and, we can add, of what is basic to life. This, at least, is what the whole transactional principle of Dewey would lead to. It would also lead to the suggestion that 'consummations akin to the esthetic' could take place only in a world something like the one we actually have. For in a world of mere change and flux, no movement would ever come to a climax, nor could any closure be more than a simple stoppage—if even that could have any meaning. There could be no tension or struggle, no resistance to be overcome. And in a world already and forever complete, fulfillment would be equally meaningless and 'change' but a dreary treadmill affair. Nor could culmination prove itself a preparation for future process: sleep would be indistinguishable from waking. But 'because the actual world, that in which we live, is a combination of movement and culmination, of breaks and re-union, the experience of a living creature is capable of esthetic quality . . . Inner harmony is attained only when, by some means, terms are made with the environment.' (11:17)

These conclusions may all be implicit in the definition of experience-as-transaction, but they are being made explicit here for at least two reasons. One is to anticipate a subsequent discussion of the naturalistic basis of Dewey's theory of value, a crucial item in his general philosophy. The other is to underscore the continuity without which his attempted delineation of *an* experience loses its deepest significance. Indeed it is the *restoration* of continuity to experience that Dewey regards as his prime task, the restoration of unity 'between the refined and intensified forms of experience that are works of art and the everyday events, doings, sufferings that are universally recognized to constitute [ordinary] experience.' (11:3) Somehow these have fallen apart; and just as it is considered by some a gross travesty to talk of the high affairs of art in terms of their organic and infra-organic foundations, so by others 'esthetic' is felt to suggest the precious and upper class, a matter not of everyday affairs but of the insulated world of museum and concert hall. So much so that a man might actually resent being told that his poking the fire gave him an esthetic experience or that his backyard garden was truly a work of art.

Dewey recognizes that nothing less than a history of culture and morals would account for the split between philistine and dilettante, for the isolation of art as something foreign and suspect, what happens in women's clubs and on Sunday afternoons as we are whisked past rows of 'great pictures.' But without such a history, it can at least be noticed that the compartmentalizing and institutionalizing of so much of modern life has tended to draw lines around its various sectors and so to fragment what otherwise might 'unite to tell a common and enlarged story.' The arts, as Santayana put it, are reserved for the holiday world, and the rest of experience can then be accepted for the dreary thing it must be.

However, it would be less than honest not to point out that in Dewey's closing chapters of *Art as Experience* he takes account of a veritable artistic revolution which was beginning to make itself felt. Exemplified perhaps most strikingly in the fields of architecture and functional design, this was a powerful movement to capture from that holiday world some of its treasures. Happily, in the almost quarter of a century since Dewey wrote so scathingly of the unholy schism between art and life—a break not much antedating the late Renaissance—the world of the arts has been finding its way back into the home, the classroom, the factory, and even the bank. Whether or not such a revolution can be attributed in part directly to Dewey is a matter of conjecture, but there can be no conjecture about his influence in making the arts an integral part of all education or in helping to extend the impact of the arts from the school and college to the entire social community.

In any event it is the breaking apart of experience, the separation of the allegedly 'normal' from the esthetically and suspect 'abnormal,' that Dewey is challenging. His constant appeal to continuity—a continuity based on the very structure of nature itself—is a formidable attempt to ground and, as it were, to justify the promise of human consciousness. But continuity is not a fetish or a magic talisman or something merely metaphysical. In the present context it will furnish an important clue to the meaning of fully realized experience—to which we must now return.

We have already indicated that integral experience is an unfractured whole, that its hangs together, that it is a situation dominated by a pervasive component quality. Quality is not something gratuitously added to an experience, attached to it as a kind of embellishment or postscript. It is a constitutive aspect. Thus, it is no surprise that the arts would furnish the most apt illustration of what is intended. 'A painting is said to have quality,' Dewey writes in the *Logic* (14:70), 'or a particular painting to have a Titian or Rembrandt quality. The word thus used most certainly does not refer to any particular line, color, or part of the painting. It is something that affects and modifies all the constituents of the picture and all of their relations.* Every detail of the painting is permeated with and determined by its quality. If we show a series of reproductions of Gothic cathedrals with one of them boasting a picture window, we should see without difficulty what is wrong, just as we would with a series of ranch houses, the last one embellished with a rose window. The quality of, say, an impressionistic painting would collapse with the introduction of an item of static realism or of explosive expressionism, for it is the very meaning of quality that it operate so as to regulate and control, to select and reject. Everything fits together as a unit: this fitting together is its quality.†

* Compare also Dewey's paper on 'Qualitative Thought,' reprinted in *Philosophy and Civilization*, Minton, Balch, New York, 1931.

† In this connection I should like to call attention to two as yet unpublished doctoral dissertations which make a distinct contribution to the discussion of quality and situation. They are N. L. Champlin's 'Controls in Qualitative Thought' (1952) and F. T. Villemain's 'The Qualitative Character of Intelligence' (1952), both on file at Columbia University. Their general point is that qualities can act as esthetic controls (chiefly of the end-means relationship) just as theories act as controls in scientific inquiry.

Although something like a painting may provide the most appropriate example, an everyday situation also has intrinsic, immediate, and total quality of one sort or other. If a shortstop starts to play a harmonica during a tense infield situation, or a lecturer in the classroom suddenly breaks into a waltz, the quality is shattered and the experience falls apart. Of course the break may be deliberate and the results, funny or hysterical as the case may be, carefully calculated. The point is simply that every situation has its own peculiar quality, its direct and unitary character, and that here is a guide to experience in its integrity. Unfortunately, much of experience is fragmented; its fractures are compound ones. We react jerkily to 'this' and 'that' and do not see the forest for the trees. We respond to 'objects,' which are an abstracted element of an entire pattern, rather than to the situation itself. Not that there is anything 'wrong' about this, or that objectification itself is not central for certain specified purposes. But when pervading quality is lost, experience necessarily loses its unified character and begins to disintegrate.

Quality is temporal as well as spatial, as is all transaction. The fusion of elements into a total pattern is, as it were, vertical as well as horizontal, with time as the longitudinal factor. A marriage of past and future in the present—what Dewey regards as primarily the task of the imagination—adds another dimension to the quality of an integrated experience; whereas inauthentic experience is that in which, among other disruptions, present is sacrificed to future or

---

Application of such an idea has already been made by the writers, chiefly in education and the behavioral sciences, and it would seem to suggest an extension and, at certain points, a possible reconstruction of Dewey's general theory of experience.

to past and temporal disintegration becomes part of a general incoherence. 'Only when the past ceases to trouble and anticipations of the future are not perturbing is a being wholly united with his environment and therefore fully alive. Art celebrates with peculiar intensity the moments in which the past reenforces the present and in which the future is a quickening of what now is.' (11:18) *An* experience is a consummation, but it is also anticipatory, intervening as well as ultimate, a matter of both end and means. A situation is a space-time affair and so its pervading quality is necessarily more than one-dimensional.

Dewey has suggested his own use of the word 'situation' probably antedated that of 'field' in modern physical theory. Whether this is the case or not, the term plays a conspicuous part in his thinking and is by no means confined to the present description of integrated experience. 'Situation,' like 'field,' implies a range. It 'stands for something inclusive of a large number of diverse elements existing across wide areas of space and long periods of time, but which, nevertheless, have their own unity.' In the present context, the use of 'situation' is testimony to a recognition that experiences 'overlap,' that each 'contains within itself something that points to other experiences.' Thus, 'situation' is a symbol for the contextual character of experience, for the fact that 'there is always a *field* in which observation of *this* or *that* object or events occurs.' (14:67) Field, transaction, context, situation—these are all verbal attempts to denote experience and to push it beyond the familiar confines of atomic minds reacting jerkily to atomic things.

But it is time to recognize that such verbal attempts must prove inadequate. We have said earlier that there is nothing esoteric or pretentious about the quality of a situation, but here we must be prepared to add that quality-and-situation remain essentially incommunicable and untranslatable. Quality 'is not something that can be expressed in words for it is something that must be *had*.' (14:70) 'No word can describe or convey a *quality*. This statement is, of course, as true of the quality *indeterminate* as it is of the qualities *red, hard, tragic,* or *amusing*. The words used can at best only serve to produce in hearer or reader an experience in which the quality mentioned is directly had or experienced.' (17:328) Thus, quality is a matter of direct confrontation, as is situation; a matter of immediate, nondiscursive experience. We can use here what term we will, something like 'intuition' or the more respectable 'insight' or even the quite academic yet increasingly fashionable 'phenomenological.' In any case, the point is the same: the final feel of a total situation is not an item of discourse or of knowledge.

Not that there is anything mysterious about an approach like this, and certainly there is nothing vague. Indeed, it has become a rather familiar recognition in esthetics that the arts are autonomous in the sense that they are not reducible to something else or even to one another. What is said via the symbolism of music is not directly translatable into other media. A poem is what it is and does not mean something else. Or, to quote the well-known line, 'this, sir, is not a woman; it is a picture.' The quality that gives art its autonomy also makes it fundamentally incommunicable in another language. It is itself—and so is the experiential situation. There is not much more we can say about it, for knowing here is ostensive; it is an affair of acquaintance, not of description.

But, then, why all this emphasis by Dewey on the quality of an experience, especially since there is so little to say about it? There are a number of reasons. One of them is indicated in the distinction just made between two kinds of knowledge, or, more accurately, between those parts of experience that are 'had' and those that are 'known.' True, these two phases function together rhythmically—we move constantly from one to the other; but they are nonetheless different, and to confuse the two is a serious error. For example, Dewey's whole approach to esthetics has been mistakenly understood as an attempt to bring the arts within the scope of his pragmatism, and the attempt has been shown—by Croce, for one—to be an unsuccessful and misguided one. But, in his direct answer to Croce,* Dewey makes this most revealing statement: 'The actual fact is that I have consistently treated the pragmatic theory as a theory of *knowing*, and as confined within the limits of the field of specifically cognitive subject-matter. And in addition I have specifically rejected the idea that aesthetic subject-matter is a form of knowledge, and have held that a prime defect of philosophies of art has been treating subject-matter as if it were . . . a kind of knowledge of Reality . . .'

This distinction is not a contribution to dualism, in the sense that dualism calls up an experience divided into different sections and located in watertight compartments. The difference between having and knowing is rather one of office and function, of phase and rhythm. The qualitative situation provides 'the background, the point of departure, and the regulative principle of all [cognitive and reflective] thinking.' There is a matrix where knowing starts and to

* *Journal of Aesthetics and Art Criticism*, VI, 3; March 1948, pp. 207–8.

which it returns. And there is a reason for the genesis of knowing, for the fact that one aspect of experience gives over to another: it is, of course, that the situation itself becomes problematic and indeterminate and requires some kind of restoration. Here will be found the very meaning of 'pragmatism'—which will occupy us at length later on.

What we are concerned with here, is the interaction between the instrumental (knowing) and the intrinsic (quality), which can lead Dewey to regard science itself as a 'handmaiden' conducting natural events to their consummation, to their 'happy issue.' 'The difference between the esthetic and the intellectual is . . . one of the places where emphasis falls in the constant rhythm that marks the interaction of the live creature with his surroundings.' However, it needs to be pointed out again that 'interaction' is not the happiest of terms, since it might indicate a more or less decisive split between the instrumental and the intrinsic, the one being 'merely' a tool and therefore probably vulgar, and the other absolutely and immaculately final. Whereas, for Dewey, means and ends are themselves aspects of a transaction rather than separate entities involved in a somewhat precarious affinity. Take, for example, the relation between these two in a work of art. Here the end pervades the means just as it does in any qualitative situation. It would be entirely out of place to say that a certain brush stroke or a particular use of color was 'merely' a means of achieving something else—the picture. True, now this and now that aspect of a painting or of a poem needs to receive a special stress, and one may even distinguish between the 'intellectual' and the 'esthetic' elements—but only as 'the place where emphasis falls.'

The rhythm of genuinely creative or appreciative experience is not broken by the shift between means and end, for means here are never 'merely' means nor are ends superlatively and aloofly set off by themselves. Means too often denote drudgery and philistine efficiency, just as ends may call up the unapproachably ideal. This cannot be the case in a fully realized experience; indeed, the quality of such an experience is precisely that it is never 'merely' anything. It is not cognitive, nor is it contemplative in the sense of being an arrest or a dislocation of experience; nor even is it 'esthetic' in that it connotes something discretely precious and rare. Quality demands wholeness, continuity, fusion; there is no falling apart, not even into end and means—(or, more accurately, 'especially' not into end and means.) '. . . All the cases in which means and ends are external to one another are non-esthetic. This externality may even be regarded as a definition of the non-esthetic.' (11:198)

It is more than this. The very problem of experience is located in the relation of the final and the instrumental, a relation, Dewey finds, which has been clearly recognized in the history of philosophy. There is a momentous chapter in *Experience and Nature*—the ninth, 'Experience, Nature, and the Arts'—in which Dewey addresses himself to such a relationship, with particular emphasis on the way in which 'art' unifies and illuminates experience. He is, of course, using the term in its broadest sense so that it includes 'making' and 'doing' as well as receiving and appreciating, and stands therefore as 'the sole alternative to luck.' This striking contrast between the designed and the fortuitous will help us understand the overpowering significance Dewey puts upon the solidarity of end and means.

We need to remember the precarious surroundings of

the live creature and that he is 'everywhere exposed to the incidence of unknown forces and hurried fatally to unforeseen consequences.' Some of these consequences are indeed eminently satisfactory—and then we are lucky. But luck is capricious, and even when it is good it carries with it the very fear of being lucky. 'We may indeed enjoy the goods the gods of fortune send us, but we should recognize them for what they are, not asserting them to be good and righteous *altogether*.' (7:372) To be good altogether, an experience needs to include control of the causal conditions that enter into it as well as celebration of the final happy results. This is art. Magic is the exclusive concern with uncontrolled hoped-for consequences, philistine drudgery, the hypnotic refusal to look beyond the means themselves. Thus, there is the uneasy oscillation between 'merely' useful arts, which become routine, and 'merely' final ends, which are then no more than distractions.

What Dewey is saying here is that art cuts through these too familiar distinctions between the instrumental and the consummatory, the practical and the theoretical, the mechanical and the immediate; and that it relocates the distinctions so that they can now be seen to be those between experiences which are full of enjoyed meanings and those which are not. This is the difference between authentic and inauthentic experience.

The enemies of the esthetic are neither the practical nor the intellectual. They are the humdrum; slackness of loose ends; submission to convention in practice and intellectual procedure. Rigid abstinence, coerced submission, tightness on one side and dissipation, incoherence and aimless indulgence on the other, are deviations in opposite direction from the unity of an experience. (11:40)

Experience as Art

It is the unity of experience which is Dewey's constant concern. Were we in a position to continue with an examination of his technical esthetics, we should find that even here the same rejection of dualism holds, as, for example, in his repudiation of the classic opposition of substance and form. These, too, are aspects of a single rhythm and not two discrete entities adventitiously coming together. Continuity can be broken even in the arts. When this happens—and it can happen for a number of reasons—the tedious debate between the vulgarian and the dilettante appears, while much of art becomes hollow and sterile, an affair only of the museum. It is these breaks which Dewey is deploring, whether they are extreme or minor. His whole argument is to the effect that there is no clear cleavage between the esthetic and the unesthetic. Experience becomes rich and valid and authentic when it illustrates appreciative perception and ordered doing, when it is shot through with pervasive total component quality; yet it is *experience* that is being appreciated, ordered, and integrated, not something else. 'Mountain peaks do not float unsupported; they do not even just rest upon the earth. They *are* the earth in one of its manifest operations.' Just as manifestly is art 'the living and concrete proof that man is capable of restoring consciously, and thus on the plane of meaning, the union of sense, need, impulse and action characteristic of the live creature.' [11:3,25]

The relation between Dewey's celebration of an integrated experience and the place of values in his philosophy ought to be apparent by now. In fact, the relation between artistic living and values in any man's philosophy ought to be equally clear. For when moralists come to define the good life, what they seem finally to reach is, in Irwin Edman's phrase, 'lucid and radiant immediacy.' Intrinsic goods and ultimate values, from Plato to Whitehead and even Russell, have always been seen in terms of esthetic appreciation, even by the ascetic. The words may sometimes obscure what is 'lucid and radiant' in the moralist's vision, but never entirely. Just so, not even sentimentality can obscure the profound appeal of the beauty-good-truth trilogy. These remarks may seem remote from the work of John Dewey, but they are not. It is true that his *theory* of value is an intricate, original, and controversial one, and it needs elaboration in a following chapter; but the unity of experience, the restoration of a synthesis of 'sense, need, impulse and action,' the striving for enjoyed meanings as the game is played through—these are what Dewey finds good.

Similarly, the relation between Dewey's sensitivity to the essentially incommunicable and nondiscursive quality of an experience and the private moral consciousness should also be apparent. The notion that his philosophy is somehow so social and groupy that the solitary experience of the individual is passed over is simply another of the stereotypes. Not that Dewey is therefore a kind of existentialist reveling in an anxious loneliness! His interest in problem solving would hardly allow that. Yet his at times passionate insistence on the immediacy and untranslatability of the consummated situation is full testimony to his regard for privacy.

It is also testimony to his regard for the truly religious dimension of man's life. In his *A Common Faith,* where he makes his classic distinction between 'religion' and 'religious,' Dewey also argues that 'religious experience' is no more a special kind of experience than is esthetic or moral experience. It is the name given to a quality, describing the effect produced, 'not the manner and cause of its production.' That quality, of course, is the one we have been endeavoring to present throughout this whole argument, what Dewey here calls 'the organic plentitude of our being.' This may occur in 'many significant moments of living,' and when it does, 'a definitely religious attitude' emerges. And it is this kind of experience, achieved perhaps most successfully by way of the fine arts, that sets the measure of a civilization. More than that: it sets the measure of the good life. For 'imagination is the chief instrument of the good' and 'art is more moral than moralities.' Indeed 'were art an acknowledged power in human association and not treated as the pleasuring of an idle moment or as a means of ostentatious display, and were morals understood to be identical with every aspect of value that is shared in experience, the "problem" of the relation of art and morals would not exist.' (11:348) It exists because man has accepted the illusion that experience can be carved up into this and that. When that illusion disappears, a unified experience will emerge as the prime human value.

3. The Nature of Value

We have been saying that integrated experience provides for John Dewey a clue to human value. But to say this is to do nothing less than open up the central problem in any philosophy, and to open it up precipitously. Even if a person sympathizes with what Dewey understands by integrated experience, he may well be led to ask: 'But is such an experience really good?' And when that question is asked, on what basis can it be answered? Will not further explanation be met by a similar question—'but is *that* truly good?' This quandary is regarded by most philosophers as the very definition of the problem of ethics, and by many contemporary philosophers it is also regarded as unanswerable, at least in the terms in which it is asked.

As usual, Dewey is not quite prepared to accept the terms in which such a question is customarily asked, since questions about the 'Good' have a tendency to keep pushing back to some infinite regress and so to find themselves at last quite outside the very situation in which questions need to be answered. The terms which indicate—at least to Dewey—the truly fundamental dimensions of ethics and human decision are those provisionally set forth in his brilliant passage on luck. It will be remembered that although 'we may indeed enjoy the goods the gods of fortune send us . . . we should recognize them for what they are, not asserting them to be good and righteous *altogether*.' To be good 'altogether' requires art, where control of conditions goes hand in hand with the memorializing of results. Dewey notices that 'primitive innocence does not last. Enjoyment ceases to be a datum and becomes a problem.' Appreciation soon turns into questioning, and between these two develops an entire rhythm of experience, the shift—already noted—between the consummatory and the instrumental, the 'perchings' and the 'flights.' 'After the first dumb, formless experience of a thing as a good, subsequent perception of the good contains at least a germ of critical reflection.' (7:401) Indeed, the immediate enjoyment itself involves at least an unwitting choice, since it indicates that some things have already been selected and others rejected, if only capriciously and arbitrarily. As Dewey recognizes, in any liking there must be *concern* or we are reduced to 'bare animal appetition' with no opportunity for judgment to emerge.

There is then no insulated wall between the immediate and the reflective in human experience. More exactly, no aspect of experience is exclusively a matter of feeling or of knowing, any more than there can normally be pure sensation devoid of all perceptual or associational elements. Experience is of a piece and is not bifurcated in some essential way; nonetheless it has a kind of double aspect and vibrates between the 'that' and the 'what,' between the esthetic and the analytical, yet with each aspect participating in the other. As an example, take the relation between the quality of a situation and its meaning. To say, as Dewey has said, that quality is what it is and therefore is indescribable is not to say that it is meaningless. On the contrary, meaning—which certainly involves the reflective and the analytical—may be the surest way of establishing and enhancing quality. Take the ordinary meaninglessness of a game of cricket for an American. The quality that emerges on the cool green oval with the white-clad players for the Englishman does not emerge for the American—unless and until he begins to understand what the game is all about. To be sure, there will probably be some immediate esthetic reaction to this situation of summer and sport; moreover, it cannot be entirely meaningless, for even the American will recognize it as a game, as a fundamental part of English culture, and perhaps even as a way of life. But when its rules and history are grasped, the *quality* of the cricket situation begins truly to be appreciated. Quality may be beyond discourse, but not beyond discourse are the conditions that make it possible. The quality of a work of art is in no way independent of knowledge of the art form: a Bach fugue will surely evoke from a sensitive listener emotive and affective reactions of a kind, but the quality of these reactions will be enriched by even an elementary familiarity with counterpoint. Meaning leads to, not away from, quality.

Similarly, quality attaches itself to meaning. Dewey has already pointed out that scientific inquiry itself must have an esthetic tone or it becomes mere routine, just as, on the other hand, the cultivation of sheer, isolated immediacies can degenerate into irresponsible posturing. The binary character of experience (which certainly has been empirically established in the course of modern psychology, whatever the school), the rhythmic interplay between the emotive and the critical, permeates all experience. This is what Dewey is constantly trying to tell us, and this is why he will reject the popular dualism which sets off, say, art and morals from science. He rejects it because art, morals, and science 'alike exhibit the difference between immediate goods casually occurring and immediate goods which have been reflectively determined by means of critical inquiry.

If bare liking is an adequate determination of values in one case, it is in the others. If intelligence, criticism, is required in one, it is in the others.' (7:407) The split in experience is not between quality and meaning, end and means, art and science, morals and technology; it is between experience that is full, ordered, and reflective and that which is fragmentary, casual, and blind.

In the above quotation the word 'values' appears. This is a key term not only in Dewey's thinking but in all contemporary philosophy, in which theory of value has become almost a separate discipline. The usual difficulty in trying to settle upon a meaning for 'value' is complicated by Dewey himself, since he has not always been precise in his use of the word. In fact, there are some statements of his which appear to suggest a position exactly contrary to what is ordinarily and correctly attributed to him.* Despite this handicap, the theory Dewey presents has been remarkably consistent over a period which includes some of his earliest and latest writings.

To indicate some of the problems involved in trying to determine what 'value' stands for (and confining ourselves to the course of current philosophy), we can simply list the following attitudes:

Item: The word is indefinable, as is 'good.' Indeed, the

* In the present context it would be pedantic to trace some of these terminological difficulties, but it might be helpful to call attention to an excellent handling of this and other problems in Dewey's theory of value in Benjamin Wolstein's 'Experience and Valuation: A Study in John Dewey's Naturalism' (1949), an unpublished doctoral dissertation available through the Columbia University Library.

two terms are almost interchangeable in their essential meaninglessness.*

Item: What is desired automatically has value. Any interest in x imputes a value to x.

Item: A value is merely an exclamation or ejaculation, a direct expression of a feeling or emotion; thus it is not really a matter for ethics at all but rather for psychology, or perhaps for rhetoric or grammar, since to say, 'Stealing is bad,' is to do no more than to say, 'Stealing,' in a certain tone of voice and with a particular facial expression, or to write 'stealing' and follow it by an appropriate mark of punctuation.

Item: An amendment to this so-called emotive theory is that values are hortatory or persuasive in character. It is not enough merely to say, 'Stealing! !'; there must also be implied, 'This is how I or we feel and you should feel likewise.' †

In one form or another, some of them quite subtle and others almost gross, this general identifying of value with sheer emotional expression is fairly current among contemporary philosophers. We might therefore introduce Dewey's interpretation of value by way of its relations,

* At times even Dewey seems to talk as if this were his position. 'Values are values, things immediately having certain intrinsic qualities. Of them as values there is accordingly nothing to be said; they are what they are.' (7:396)

† The works referred to in this inventory would include, for example: G. E. Moore, *Principia Ethica*, Cambridge University Press, Cambridge, 1st ed., 1903; R. B. Perry, *General Theory of Value*, Longmans, Green, New York, 1926; A. J. Ayer, *Language, Truth, and Logic*, Victor Gollancz, London, 2nd ed., 1946 (1st ed., 1936); C. L. Stevenson, *Ethics and Language*, Yale University Press, New Haven, 1945.

positive and negative, to such an identity. His statement that 'enjoyment ceases to be a datum and becomes a problem' provides a good take-off point. For it calls attention, first, to the fact that there are indeed things and actions which men seek to enjoy and which they therefore hold dear and prize; but it also calls attention to the sad fact that some things which men seek to enjoy conflict with other things. It would be embarrassing to give illustrations, so familiar is this conflict. Equally familiar is the all-too-frequent incompatibility between what is desired and what, for various reasons, 'ought' to be desired, i.e. the desirable. What we want, therefore, may do no more than set up a problem. Indeed, 'want' itself signifies that something is wanting, is missing; the situation is incomplete; were everything stabilized, as with a replete oyster in its bed, desire and want would have no meaning. But putting that aside we still need to ask the question: Is desire (or whatever term be used) *sufficient* to account for the appearance of value? That it is *necessary* in explaining value, Dewey, of course, accepts; but he cannot accept the contention that desires or 'goods' are automatically values.

Desires and goods are what they are—immediate, noncognitive experiences. But a value, Dewey insists, is something else. It is the result of a judgment, however simple. 'Value' is a noun established by the verb or action of e-valuating. It begins to originate when the immediately enjoyed object becomes suspect, when it begins to cloy, when some other object of enjoyment begins to compete for recognition. It is when a liking for the jukebox has to meet the competition of the symphony orchestra (say, on the radio or television) that a problem arises. And when a problem arises, another dimension is introduced.

Whether 'value' should be used for this other dimension, Dewey professes to be a minor matter; but it is not a minor matter to distinguish between mere likings and those that make a claim upon our conduct; it is not a minor matter to separate the *de facto* from the *de jure*. In a way, this is what the whole question is about. Evaluation is a search for the connection between things, between the simple lauding or celebration of what we like and the conditions of their manifestation. There can be no *theory* of immediate enjoyments, but there can be—indeed, there must be—a theory of the choice among enjoyments.

Let us approach this distinction in another way by asking whether values and emotive expressions are identical. By identity we mean, is the proposition directly convertible or reversible, so that 'if all values are emotive expressions,' then 'all emotive expressions are values'? The first of these may be acceptable, but what about the second? Its assertion would seem to imply a failure to distinguish between exclamations or ejaculations as simple items of organic behavior, like a baby's gurgle or squeal, and the application of this largely spontaneous behavior as a sign. Dewey expresses it this way: 'A baby cries. The mother takes the cry as a sign the baby is hungry or that a pin is pricking it, and so acts to change the organic condition inferred to exist by using the cry as an evidential sign.'* Organic behavior is what it is. It is very often random and exploratory, and, without making certain quite dubious assumptions, it cannot necessarily be regarded as *expressing* anything, much less something as complicated as an emotion. But, letting that pass, it would appear that an exclamation cannot also

* *Theory of Valuation, International Encyclopaedia of Unified Science,* Vol. II, No. 4, University of Chicago Press, Chicago, 1939, p. 8.

be regarded as a value unless it functions as a symbol, as part of what is clearly a social situation. This is the point that Dewey is making, and others, too, for example George Mead and the contemporary interpersonal psychiatrists. As part of a social situation, e.g. baby's cry and mother's intervention, an exclamation can be regarded as a proposition which (a) can be judged true or false—e.g. the young boy feigning sickness to avoid school—and which (b) does or does not produce results—the mother comes to the aid of the child or she doesn't; the boy escapes school, or not. What Dewey is urging, then, is simply this: immediate likings or emotive expressions present themselves as *candidates* for value status; they achieve that status when they come to stand as significant symbols in a problem situation and thus serve to resolve the problem.

But problems, it will be pointed out, may be 'solved' in several ways. We can lie down till the feeling passes over, or not look and maybe the problem will go away. Then there are always habit, impulse, and improvisation. But is there a 'right' way to solve problems? And, if there is, is it possible that this may be the direction in which to look for a theory of value which ventures to go beyond emotional ejaculation?

To answer this with both bluntness and tautology, the only 'good' solution to a problem is one which indeed solves it without still further enlarging the problem. To jump into a snowbank to quench a fever, or to burn down houses in order to secure roast pig, would be to aggravate rather than to solve a problem. Use of an ordinary monkey wrench instead of a pipe wrench may open or close a fitting, but only at the expense of both tool and pipe. Now these illustrations are clearly not moral ones, even if adjectives like 'good,' 'better,' or 'proper' may apply. This suggests the possibility that an effective and neutral approach to a theory of value as problem-solving might be a general one applicable to all problematic situations, not simply to those designated as value situations. In other words, is there any connection between value judgments and 'practical' judgments?

A practical judgment, for Dewey, is one applying to specific, incomplete, problematic, objective situations (objective, of course, does not exclude the maker of the judgment); situations in which, as with the self-fulfilling prophecy, the proposition plays a part, even if a minor one, in the completion of the situation. Thus, a practical proposition is one dealing *hypothetically* with a predictive future.

Almost fifty years ago Dewey tried to develop the 'logic of judgments of practice.' (4:Chap. XIV) Illustrations of such judgments are almost embarrassingly familiar. 'You had better consult a psychiatrist.' 'This is a good time to build a house.' 'The United States ought constantly to reexamine its foreign policy.' 'You would be wrong to consult another physician.' What is meant by calling these 'practical'? For one thing, they indicate that something needs to be done or not done. This, in turn, suggests that the situation in question is an incomplete or unresolved one—which, of course, is why we call it problematic. The situation itself is incomplete or unresolved, not simply the mind of the subject. If I judge that I should or should not contribute money for the election of *X*, I am not simply making a subjective judgment. The situation itself is fluid and unsettled, for the election has not yet been decided; it will be decided one way or the other; *X*'s party needs money. These and many other conditions are independent of my judgment, but they are factors in the judgment just as I am myself. These conditions indicate the situation to be unfinished and problematic.

Further, they indicate that my own judgment and my subsequent action will be a factor, however small, in completing or resolving the situation. *X*'s party will or will not get my financial help, and this may be a factor, again however small, in determining the election. If it were not, there would be no problem! Contrast this with other situations which, even if incomplete, are not affected by my judgment or action: 'It is about to snow.' 'He is already on his way to Chicago.' 'The path of hurricane Janet is still undetermined.'

Now, how does this analysis of a certain kind of problem-directed judgment apply to value? Why does Dewey hold that values are an executive example of judging activity? To answer these, and to begin to prepare also an answer for the earlier question about the good, it may be well to make a fresh start.

The question that Dewey is trying to answer throughout is, How do things or acts or events come to have value? The assumption behind this question is, of course, that values are neither immediate nor indefinable (which is not to deny that there may be undefined fundamentals basic to any definition). Instead, values are looked upon as the outcome of a process of selection and arise when our unreflective appreciations are in some way challenged. We have, then, a second-level phenomenon, one more abstract and more of a logical construct than the sheer likings between which values mediate. It is for this reason, Dewey argues, that there can be a *theory* of evaluations but none of immediate enjoyments. We can rephrase the point in another way:

The Nature of Value

Values are choices, man's long-time decisions in the general areas encompassing his basic attitudes, his deep-rooted interests, his objects of respect and reverence. These choices —which have also been called ends and standards—arise in the context of ongoing activity. They are not antecedent to that activity but emerge in the course of the transactions involving man with his surroundings.*

But how can that be? Do not choices depend upon standards and not the other way around? Is Dewey not entering the usual vicious circle? Even if the great Spinoza himself asserted that things are good because they are wanted, certainly must we not also insist that things are wanted because they are good? That there is a seeming fallacy in this mutual interdependence of choices and values, desires and goods, is undeniable; but it is no more of a barrier to discussion than the scandalous circle in which induction and deduction themselves are intertwined. Here, too, one depends upon the other, as is also the case in certain celebrated mathematical and logical paradoxes. But there is more to valid inquiry than mere circlophobia. Even the definition of words is ordinarily circular despite the fact that one of the traditional rules for good definition denies it. What good definitions—and thinking—do, however, is to widen the circle of meaning, or, if it is not bad geometry, to

* Charles Morris in *Varieties of Value* urges that 'value' be regarded as a complex term which includes at least three different things. One is what he calls 'operative,' a matter of preference as is here outlined. Another is 'conceived' value, such as that of a drug addict who knows that his compulsion is not valuable even when he chooses it. Thirdly, there is 'object' value, what is held to be a desirable, whether preferred or not, such as a correct diet. These are clearly different things and whether the same term can apply to all of them is one of the difficulties of contemporary value theory.

change the circle into a spiral. Thus, words or ideas become richer and more significant when they are placed in larger contexts, and it is such an expansion of meaning and broadening of perspective that finally breaks the circle, or, at least, its vicious parts.

The same process of enlargement applies to values. To say a thing has value because it is wanted, and wanted because it is valuable, may seem naïve if not worse. But it is, as a matter of fact, a realistic observation accounting for the fact that choice is fundamental in the establishment of value, but that the choice is not made in a vacuum. When a man prefers *X* to *Y* in any dimension of his experience, he is not starting afresh with nothing to go by. On the contrary, he has at hand an entire system of mores, of choices, of already determined cultural choices. When he is tempted to kill someone, he does not have to start from scratch. Judgments are made against the setting of the entire history of human choices, and as this setting comes into prominence behavior is chosen because it is 'good.' But just as surely do goods depend upon wants, for it is only when a man performs the act of decision—and in no other way—that he sets up the operating values of his life. To ask which has priority is no different from the old chicken-and-egg business. The *process* of evaluation is a constant to-and-fro process, like all thinking; it is neither a simple nor a vicious circumscription. The very movement of the process makes it grow beyond the limits of any circle.

A similar extension of meaning is applicable to the uneasy relation between end and means, a problem we have already met in Dewey's discussion of esthetic quality. His long-time attempt to reduce the end-means dislocation is one of the notable elements of his philosophy—perhaps 'notorious' is the word, since it tends to contravene a distinction than which none is more popular and plausible. Ends, it seems almost universally agreed, are intrinsic and antecedent, while means are merely instrumental to given ends. And values are a matter of ends, not of means. Thus, it is said, not education or even intelligence can be a value since they are exploited by all kinds of people, bad as well as good. Ends are immediate and final, exempt from the manipulation appropriate to means.

But take some supposedly final end, say, love, or even the esthetic experience. Such an end is not simply lauded by those who claim it to be intrinsic. It has to be made effectual and meaningful, discriminations must be recognized, relations need to be discovered or improved. Without these connections, the most honorific end becomes as trivial as our most irresponsible daydream: we wish to be a great musician—but not to practice; to be a world-famous scientist—but without mathematical training; to lose weight—without dieting. These may be juvenile and even innocent ways of passing time in our heads, but they surely provide no model for value theory! At the risk of seeming arbitrary, one may insist that there is *nothing at all* final or intrinsic in the sense of being out of context or out of relation. Certainly one can be even more confident in the case of 'end,' which would seem to be at least as relational and as logically dependent upon means as are cognate concepts like cause and effect.

It must be apparent at this point that the term 'end' is not self-explanatory, for it means at least several things. There is, for instance, the simple meaning of a limit, the stop or *finis* of a problem or a process. This may be only a pun, yet some of the difficulties of the notion of 'final end' or 'end-in-itself' might be removed if this temporal or periodic sense were really taken seriously. That is to say, natural processes do start and stop, a point noted earlier in our discussion of the natural rhythms directing the very cadence of experience. A natural end is a pause, great or small, where an event comes to a period, or at least to a semicolon. Some of these natural beginnings and endings favor man, others do not. The rhythms of nature are what they are: to man they can be beneficial, neutral, malignant. To regard *all* natural processes as exclusively good, bad, or supremely indifferent is blatantly anthropomorphic. But to regard man—himself a natural process, evolving and growing in a world made neither for him nor to thwart him in some conspiratorial fashion—as a dynamic, interacting factor, choosing among the other serial events around him in order to survive and develop, is to discover why some natural endings *become* ends-in-view and others, ends-to-be-rejected—so, values and disvalues. The process of choosing, or evaluation, is thereby established, a process no less natural because it is human.

What about 'end-in-view'? Take, as Dewey does, the example of a physician treating a patient:

> He forms ends-in-view . . . on the ground of what his examination discloses is the 'matter' or 'trouble' with the patient. He estimates the worth of what he undertakes on the ground of its capacity to produce a condition in which these troubles will not exist . . . But he does not have an idea of health as an absolute end-in-itself, an absolute good by which to determine what to do . . . There is no need to deny that a general and abstract conception of health finally develops. But it is the outcome of a great number of definite, empirical inquiries, not an a priori preconditioning 'standard' for carrying on inquiries.*

* *Theory of Valuation,* op. cit. p. 46.

This is a most important passage. It indicates the very heart of an experimentalist philosophy, for it suggests that ends and standards (values) are formed in the very process of problem solving. Here ends signify clearly ends-in-view, the consequences of specified procedures, not something absolute and grandly out of context. (Indeed, an absolute may well be defined as that which has no context.) Another phrasing of the same point would underscore the if-then character of the relationship between means and end: *if* this particular illness is to be overcome, *then* this or that needs to be done. Now, it may seem that this kind of if-then or hypothetical relationship is simply swimming in vacancy and anchored nowhere, since there must be at least one ultimate—Health, Life, Happiness, Rightness, or some other —lest this entire process of problem solving be without foundation. Even the theory of relativity depends upon a constant factor.

This complaint is, of course, crucial; two different paths may be used in approaching it. There is, first, the contextualism Dewey is pushing at this point. Here he simply denies that problem-directed questions must constantly be pushed back to some overpowering ultimate. We are constantly running in the middle lane between frantic improvisation and the final realities; and what we ought to do is in all but the most exceptional cases a matter of Dewey's "practical judgment," in which *if* this particular action is taken, *then* some predicted result should follow. The urgencies of the situation, as Sidney Hook has phrased it, dominate, not some overarching exemplar. Suppose, to use Dewey's own illustration, the problem of a contemplated suicide is involved. 'No one ever influenced a person considering committing suicide by arguments concerning the value of life,' but only by the suggestion of specific conditions and possibilities—like William James's 'wait for the next mail.' Man's value transactions are an on-going flow, and, despite the philosophers, they are not constantly interrupted by the invoking of ultimates. Is not any one of us able to corroborate this?

Yet there is another approach to the quest for finalities in which, at least implicitly, Dewey does appeal to a fundamental basis for operations, one that can be phrased in moral terms: It is good to solve problems. Professor Gail Kennedy calls this kind of assumption the hidden link in Dewey's theory of value,* since it is not usually made explicit. Dewey, like anyone else, has to rely on some primitive, undefined elements—or at least one such element—to serve as a postulational basis. If some such assumption is not accepted, then discussion ceases. For example, should someone be unwilling to entertain at least tentatively the contention that problems ought to be solved, then there is nothing more to say.

It is not quite as bald as this, however. To repeat a point made earlier, there is also the question whether there is a *right* way to solve problems. Burning down houses to roast pigs or jumping into snowbanks to quench fevers might seem to satisfy our postulate, but not adequately, since the problem remains in an exaggerated form. It would appear, then, that there is a companion postulate underlying Dewey's theory of value, and this is one which is made quite explicit. '... There is something unique in the value or goodness of reflection.' (7:403)

Is this Dewey's ultimate value? Is this—to look the other

* Cf. *Journal of Philosophy*, Vol. LII (1955), No. 4, pp. 85–94.

way—the presupposition fundamental to pragmatism? 'Ultimate,' of course, is a difficult word. If it signifies an absolute end-in-itself, abstracted from any temporal context, then the concept has been the object of some of Dewey's most sustained polemics. Reflection is certainly not understood by him in the classic sense in which Reason or the Intellect stands outside the human process, elevated over all else, say, feeling or emotion. But there is a more literal meaning in which 'ultimate' denotes coming last in a temporal series. Now, one 'is quite right in saying that for me the method of intelligent action is precisely such an ultimate value. It is the last, the final or closing, thing we come upon in inquiry into inquiry.' (Dewey in 19:594.) The point of this somewhat cryptic remark would seem to lie in the realization that what we finally reach in the analysis of valuational activity is never some overall Good or Truth, but rather the *process* by which various specific goods do emerge and begin to operate. We come upon 'the logic of practical judgments.' This process does not itself have to be reflective, since the choices leading to value can be arbitrary or whimsical; but when the process of making judgments is understood, then the possibility of options other than those of caprice and authority becomes that much more real.

What Dewey is saying is, once more, that skill is the sole alternative to luck. When conflicting wants present themselves, something has to be done—something will be done. Choice cannot be eliminated, nor can values fail to arise. Dewey is proposing that intelligent be substituted for arbitrary choice. This is not intended to be simply an honorific statement. By intelligent choice he understands the control of means in order to reach and test ends-in-view, using the funded knowledge of previous end-means relations. This is what it is to be rational, what is 'unique in the value or goodness of reflection'; it permits us to *solve* problems and not disguise them or pass them by.

All problems? Nothing that Dewey has said is to the effect that intelligence is omnicompetent. For one thing, many of our problems are indeed managed unreflectively and uncritically, and that is that. Furthermore, there well may be insoluble problems, although some of them are insoluble by definition and others by arrested analysis; still others are simply testimony to the depreciation and rejection of piecemeal solutions and the insistence that all difficulties be taken care of together and at once, which is better known as magic. All of which is not to deny that there are conflicts seemingly beyond our present competence. But such a recognition is in no way incompatible with Dewey's basic assumption that problems need to be solved and that reflection is the most adequate way to do it. This is the nub of his interpretation of value.

To rephrase the entire argument, when Dewey separates values from immediate likings or desires, he is making a distinction, but he is not trying to construct two independent dimensions of experience. If reflective valuation appears to be a prime good for Dewey, it is not the only one. In future discussions we shall see that growth, development of human capacities, the democratic reconstruction of society are also somehow goods. But no one of them is The Good—not even intelligence—since they all arise in specific contexts. Is there no master context? What could it be except 'integrated experience,' where art and reflection tend to coincide as the answers to luck, magic, and disruption? 'If we wished to transmute this generalization into a categorical imperative we should say: "So act as to increase the meaning of present experience."' (6:283)

Among the many questions which must arise from any discussion of Dewey's theory of value, there is at least one which demands further treatment. It concerns the relation of values to reflective thinking and, inevitably, to scientific method. That is to say, is Dewey serious when he suggests that men can ever think critically about their desires and conflicts? Does he feel that a scientific approach to value is really feasible? This kind of question—enormously difficult as it may be—has to be reckoned with. But before that is possible, a great deal more needs to be said about Dewey's use of thinking, knowledge, truth, science, and inquiry. It is to these we must turn before we come back again to value.

4. Inquiry, Knowing, and Truth

No more than value is knowledge an immediate or all-pervading phenomenon. Just as value emerges from a context, so knowledge comes out of a transaction that encompasses other aspects of experience. Dewey holds that experience is wider than knowledge of it, that things are *had* in advance of their being *known.* Before there is discrimination there is need of it, for even if all aspects of experience are equally real they are not equally efficacious.

These contentions fly in the face of the philosophic tradition. According to that tradition, all of man's experience is a knowledge-affair, an affair in which man looks at the world with a staring eye. This look is somehow bifocal. As he uses one lens, man seems only a passive and idle spectator peering in upon a world disinterestedly, but when he uses the other, the world is magnified and distorted in a truly remarkable manner. This distortion gives rise to the classic problem of knowledge. Dewey rejects the bifocal vision, one lens at a time. The first rejection is considered here, the second toward the close of the chapter.

At the outset Dewey challenges the traditional assumptions that experience is exhausted by the ubiquitous relation of knowing and that man knows simply by casting a vacant eye at the world, having little other communion with it. That there is constant sensitive contact between the organism and its environment, a kind of simple awareness, Dewey or no one else could deny. Such irritability or sensitivity is one of the defining factors of organic behavior.

But, for Dewey, such primary physical contact is not knowledge; rather it is the background against which the activity of knowing takes place, the matrix of knowledge. This matrix of awareness provides the opportunities and the raw materials of knowledge, but something has to happen first. As always, Dewey is concerned with genesis and growth—how does knowledge arise, what is its natural history, why does not all our experience remain a matter of 'havings' and 'enjoyments'? The quick answer, as has been noted earlier, is that incompatibilities arise within experience which force the organism to pay attention. But let us move less quickly.

The background of knowledge, Dewey avers, is the broad general field of sensitive awareness. Now, if one wishes, this can be regarded as an immediate apprehension by the organism of portions of its environment. It may be further agreed that this apprehension is affected through (or produces, as the case may be) what have been termed sensations, perceptions, and so on. Dewey demurs at the point where, according to the canon, this immediate apprehension is called knowledge. His objection is that knowledge, being a process or, more accurately, the result of a process, cannot be immediate. The process begins when one item of experience comes to stand as a sign for something beyond itself, when meanings start to emerge. A color, say, or a sound, or a dark patch in the sky, is simply what it is, like a sneeze or a basic want. It can be pointed to, but it is not a matter for discourse at all, whereas 'knowledge is a memorandum of . . . sequences, co-existences, relations.' When the sneeze leaves the realm of the reflex and is suddenly appreciated as the index of a possible cold or the presence of ragweed; when the patch in the sky is now noticed as cloud-presaging-rain; when one want collides with another—inference, in however simple a form, is under way. Unless it serve as a symbol, a sense datum is merely a candidate for knowledge, just as sheer desire is merely a candidate for value status.

The situation in which knowledge is born, according to Dewey, is a problematic one. Why a suggestion like this provokes adjectives like 'vulgar,' 'sordidly practical,' 'bourgeois,' and even 'American,' is not easy to understand. It seems almost as if a kind of pride like the Greek *hubris* prevents us from acknowledging that problems can be of all kinds and occur in all dimensions. A child's curiosity, the philosophic wonder celebrated by Plato and Aristotle, the arrangement of men on a chess-board, even the incandescent setting for Spinoza's intellectual love of God—these are hardly utilitarian, yet they all appear to arise because of some hiatus between what is immediately experienced and what is not; they arise when through signs and inference we try to tie together the less fixed and more fixed parts of experience. Unless there is to be an interdict on words like these, 'problem,' 'difficulty,' 'discrepancy,' or something of the sort would seem to be the symbol for situations in which inquiry originates.

Perhaps the word 'knowledge' is a block. It connotes something fixed, respectably established, and secure against the urgency of change—and so, it may be, genteel. In any event, Dewey prefers the active form 'knowing' and also the term 'inquiry,' a legacy from Charles Peirce. 'Knowledge' becomes then a shorthand device and stands elliptically for many specific acts. It is the terminus of inquiry. Take as an illustration the writings of so many British philosophers, in which the reader is constantly confronted with objects like chairs, pennies, desks in the study, and trees on the lawn. These are the stock scenery around which the drama of knowledge is played to its rather unconvincing dénouement. But no one of these objects constitutes a problem at all! They cannot possibly serve now as models for a *process* of inquiry, although at one time in the history of man they undoubtedly did. If the epistemologists were suddenly to find themselves in little Alice's Wonderland, they might detect what inquiry feels like. When mallets turn suddenly into flamingoes and croquet balls into hedgehogs—well, then there would be a problematic situation! It could be a revolutionary one but not necessarily vulgar.

Knowledge, then, is a kind of experience and grows out of other and wider kinds, those of immediate enjoyments and consummations—which is not to deny that the activity of knowing can itself become consummatory. It is an activity which arises when a situation of crisis appears. Such a situation—small or large—forces the organism to take into account and redirect sensory material already available, and to dig for more. Iron is dug out of the ground, but to be used it first has to be smelted and refined. By analogy, raw sensory material needs to be transformed via judgment and inference. Sensations, to change the figure, are not royal roads to knowledge, but rather signs which indicate where the road may be and to what it leads. And, since inquiry is a continuing process, the terminus of one problem is more than likely the entrance for another.

Why is this approach so uncongenial, at least to the philosophic tradition? The answer may be found in an earlier discussion of discontinuity and dualism. If indeed there are two worlds, an inner and an outer, one of mind and one of matter, of appearance and of reality; and if man is but a passive spectator viewing one world through the peep-hole of another, then perhaps all he can do is to attempt feebly and imperfectly to secure a copy of what he sees. His mind becomes a duplicating machine directed to making more or less faithful reproductions.These are called ideas. Knowing is, in consequence, not an integral part of the world but an outside and alien intruder which, for some reason or another, is bound to keep turning out facsimiles. Except for this practice—which, however, is both incorrigible and universal—the knowing mind is passive and inoperative, it does not *do* anything to the world. Finally, the reliability of these supposed facsimiles can never be discovered, and so we have the problem of Truth.

This classic syndrome of knowledge uses a number of terms, at least one of which may serve as a handle to get a firmer hold on what Dewey is proposing. This is the all-important 'idea,' without which most of modern philosophy would find itself inarticulate. The word has, to be sure, many meanings both in philosophy and out of it, but the general interpretation would seem to regard an idea as subjective, mental, something the mind makes. An idea is the object of the mind when a man thinks, says Locke, agreeing at least here with Descartes; and 'thinking' stands for all forms of consciousness. In theory of knowledge, 'idea' often has the more limited denotation of a mental image induced by stimuli from without; here it is close to 'sensation' or 'perception.' Or ideas may be entirely internal, as when we simply think or imagine. Whatever else it may refer to in the tradition, 'idea' does imply a subjective consciousness, and consciousness (except for idealists) implies a separate and private dimension cut off from the world of things.

Dewey's use of 'idea' is entirely different. It cannot be separated from the genesis of knowledge, from the problematic or indeterminate situation. His own familiar example is that of a man lost in the woods. What is needed by the lost man is a plan of action, a working hypothesis, an imaginary map indicating a possible way out of the woods. What is certainly *not* needed is a copy, however reliable, of the trees and rocks and grass surrounding the man. What *is* needed is not a photograph but a suggestion that includes other elements besides those directly perceived. If this were unnecessary, then the man would not be lost. (In fact, as someone has observed, the lost man knows very well where *he* is—right here! It's the other places, where he is not, that worry him.) So,

> the lost man has no alternative except to wander aimlessly or else to *conceive* this inclusive environment; and this conception is just what is meant by idea . . . *It is the interpretation of the locally present environment in reference to its absent position,* that part to which it is referred as another part so as to give a view of a whole. Just how such an idea would differ from one's plan of action in finding one's way, I do not know . . . It is a map constructed with one's self lost and one's self found, whether at starting or at home again, as its two limits.
>
> (4:238–9; italics in original.)

The homeliness of this example is deceiving. Dewey could easily have made it philosophically respectable by simply extending the situation, because people get lost in places other than woods—in ethics and politics, even in logic and metaphysics—and their being lost can be defined in the same way as it is in the woods: one part of the situation is out of harmony with another part. What is wanted in either case is an emergence of clues or signals pointing from a more fixed experience to a less fixed, an extension of meaning stretching from where we are to where we want to be. This kind of signification is quite unlike the mere appearance of sense data. True enough, as with any data, those of sensation are what we have to take into account; they are stimuli for knowledge, the points at which the world breaks in and, as with a sudden and unexpected clap of thunder, interrupts the customary quiet. And we may simply revel in the immediacy of the thunderous noise. But when, say, a cloudy winter sky is suddenly split by a flash and a rolling rumble, then we need to fit this strange phenomenon into a context and use it as a sign pointing beyond itself. In this case, as Dewey makes clear, the sensation is precisely what is *not* called up in the projected explanation, for it has already served its purpose. What is demanded, as in any problematic situation, is not an immediate and irreducible experience, but a candidate for knowledge. This is what he means by an idea. It gives meaning and points the way out of the wood. An idea is 'an organic anticipation of what will happen when certain operations are executed under and with respect to observed conditions.' We can add that this is also a definition of intelligence.

The traditional interpretation of the place of ideas in knowing would seem to have difficulty in explaining how intelligence does solve problems. A mere copy of an indeterminate situation could do no more than provide another indeterminate situation. This would appear to add up to meaningless activity since, as Sidney Hook has noticed, it would not be a means to anything, except possibly to overproduction. As a matter of fact, the so-called copy theory of knowledge is hardly a theory at all: it really is only a statement of what has to be explained. What has to be explained is precisely how we can escape from the alleged prison of the mind and effect a reconstruction of the situation itself. (It must be repeated that when Dewey speaks of a problematic—or, since the publication of his *Logic*, an indeterminate—situation, it is the *situation* itself which is involved and not simply the mind of the knower. If doubt were entirely subjective, reflecting nothing of a transactional relation between the doubter and his environment, it would have to be regarded as pathological.) What has to be explained is the public, active, and selective efficaciousness of ideas as they function in the actual solution of problems.

Standard epistemology overemphasized the camera analogy of knowing and underplayed the motor and behavioral elements of inquiry. What actually is done, especially in an experimental laboratory, has had little weight in establishing a model for cognition because, according to Dewey, philosophy has been hypnotized by the spectator point of view. Significant knowledge about an atom or a star, a human mind or a social system, a jellyfish or the history of your country, is in every case different from what the contemplation theory assumes. On the contrary, what is assumed is the activity tied up with Wilson cloud chambers, Geiger counters, spectroscopes, sphygmographs, statistical indices, documentary analysis, staining of tissue, and numberless other physical and operational entries to knowledge. Knowledge here is a matter of doing, not simply of beholding. Every laboratory is a scene of action, in which thumping, pulling, squeezing, however refined and subtle, become as much an integral part of the experimental process as the most exquisite pointer reading. Dewey urges that theory of knowledge be based on the way problems are really solved, especially through scientific method, rather than upon dialectical ingenuity. Here he is in complete agreement with Einstein, who, it may be remembered, advised that we pay attention not to what scientists say but to what they do. And when we pay such attention, we find the age-old distinctions between certain and uncertain, matter and mind, object and subject, becoming blurred and less plausible. The chasm separating knower from known seems less forbidding. In fact, there is no chasm at all. The knowing operation seems to be a unit, a transaction involving a knowing-known relation in which cooperation replaces the ancient competition between ideas and things. (This 'knowing-known transaction' represents Dewey's final terminology.) In any event, if what goes on in scientific inquiry is not a capital illustration of what is intended by knowing, then it is indeed difficult to understand what would be.

The transition from Dewey's theory of knowing to a theory of truth is smooth and inescapable. For we need to ask: When is knowledge trustworthy? When does an idea, a plan of action, become a valid one? Would it be accurate to say that only true beliefs constitute knowledge?

Now, any effort to answer without apology the question asked by Pontius Pilate—and not by him alone—may appear presumptuous. The reason seems clear. There is in operation a kind of word-magic that has elevated terms like

Reality, Mind, Value, Truth, and many others to such a privileged, yet non-negotiable, position that one must figuratively remove one's hat, perhaps shoes, in their presence. But the fact is that discussion is simply blocked by words like these. They represent what Dewey calls *the* philosophic fallacy, the conversion of anticipated functions into antecedent existents. At every point from now on we shall meet the same blocking of investigation by overburdened symbols. This is why, at ninety, Dewey—along with Arthur Bentley—was driven to propose a trial group of names in an attempt to remove the dead weight from words that must still be used, or to start afresh with a new and unencumbered vocabulary. In this respect at least Dewey was quite in sympathy with much of contemporary philosophic analysis.

If a countervailing stereotype could arbitrarily be set up, it should be to the effect that Dewey's interest in 'truth' was overwhelming. But his interest was not in mere lyrical commemoration of it. It was rather a strenuous, sometimes desperate, effort to say what he intended by the word, and in this he was in line with the work of his pragmatic predecessors. It will not be possible here to trace the pragmatic theory of truth back through William James and Charles Peirce, but all the American pragmatists—far apart as they are on many issues—agree that pragmatism does not start with a theory of truth. It starts with a theory of meaning and of knowledge, to which the truth doctrine stands as a corollary. Just as sensations are not themselves knowledge, nor desires, values—although these furnish the raw material for knowledge and values—so all meanings do not put in a claim to truth. 'The realm of meaning is wider than that of true-and-false meaning, it is more urgent and more fertile.' It would include poetic meaning, moral meaning, perhaps religious—'a large part of our life is carried on in a realm of meaning to which truth and falsity as such are irrelevent.' Thus, within the general range of meaning there are discriminations, of which the true-false is one. And, like the genesis of knowledge itself, the true-false discrimination originates in a problem. As Dewey has emphasized: 'The problematic situation is the context in which everything I say about knowing and truth is placed and by reference to which it is to be understood.' (19:560)

If this continued reference to problems still seems on the one hand trivial or, on the other, somehow coarse, it may be appropriate to ask for an alternative and possibly more congenial context in which truth is to appear. Such a context would probably be one in which there was little distinction between Truth and Reality. The first is a restatement of the second, existing in a special world waiting to be uncovered. In other words, truth already exists, as does reality, whether anyone comes upon it or not. It is just there. If this should seem somewhat supererogatory, then it can be supplemented by the familiar correspondence or copy theory, which is that an idea is true if it agrees with reality. Truth, then, is a duplicate of or deputy for reality. This is certainly the most popular of all explanations of truth, whether in common sense or philosophy, and it probably is what most persons would settle for. It is definitely an advance over what may be called the identity theory, for it does distinguish between truth and reality. It does not gild the lily by insisting that we have two terms, reality *and* truth, standing for the same thing. After all, what would be a false reality? And is a fact more of a fact if it is true?

Since it does make a distinction, the correspondence theory has to do with the statements men make about the world. It therefore involves meaning or discourse and refers to ideas and their validity. To this degree it is eminently plausible. But the relationship between ideas and reality is held to be one-to-one—the closer the correspondence, the more reliable or true the idea. Now, we already have had occasion to question this copy theory of truth. It faces, for example, the dualistic split between reality and appearance, between mind and matter, between the original and the copy—in fact, it simply restates the classic problem of knowledge. The theory will also have extraordinary trouble in accounting for scientific inquiry, which implies much more than the mere staring of an idle watcher. A copy interpretation of truth, finally, will still fail to explain why—especially if there be no problem—the mind should make a copy of nature in the first place. After all, to quote Virginia Woolf, 'One damned world is enough.'

Despite these handicaps, the correspondence theory has a *prima facie* appeal. Its real difficulty is that it is vague and unanalyzed. What actually does it *mean* to aver that a true idea copies reality? The pragmatic or instrumentalist approach, that of consequences, is frankly an effort to analyze the correspondence theory and to develop what it seems to be saying, which is that an idea, like a map, should lead to the results it is designed for. That these results should be to produce mirror images, even were that possible, would seem to be repudiated by the very ways in which ideas function. They function like maps. Now, a map may seem the closest thing to a copy (it is what Peirce called an 'icon,' a sign which resembled the thing signified), but it is far from a copy. No map duplicates the terrain; if it did, it would not be a map. Instead, it is a device that permits us to come into effective and fruitful relations with the terrain—to go from *X* to *Y*, I need a map; the map is reliable if, using it, I reach *Y* from *X*. Should one ask at this point how I *really know* if I am at *Y*, or whether I should be at *Y* anyhow, certainly more than a map is needed! Here is a different kind of a problem, for which (unless the problem be actually insoluble) one needs another kind of device. And should it be pointed out that maps are reliable *because* they are true, it is simply an indication that the argument has been missed. The consequences theory of truth is an aspect of *meaning*, not of scientific procedure or of morals: Dewey is trying to describe the *nature* of truth; he is not providing a substitute for the specific practices and confrontations found, in deciding what is true. These are the technical concerns of the various disciplines. In this connection, it might be significant that scentists rarely speak of truth—except when they philosophize. They speak of 'adequate' or 'fruitful' hypotheses, and of degrees of reliability, of veri-fication, i.e. 'making true.' Also they seldom speak of fact or reality, but rather of data.

What we are saying, then, is that true-false is a property of ideas (in Dewey's use of the term). This property, even if it be called loosely one of correspondence, is that of prediction—what consequences will follow if the plan of action, symbolized by the idea, is carried out. Ideas operate like hypotheses, being verified or disverified in the light of predictable results. If now it is asked, *which* results or consequences?—the only answer can be: those in terms of which a problem has arisen. 'If you tried to cut with a pencil or write with a knife,' Ernest Nagel has said, 'the plan would fail. There lies the difference between truth and error.' A knife cuts *better* than a pencil; a pencil writes *better* than a knife. Does 'better' mean subjective or emotional satisfaction? Not at all. The prediction that a knife will write well, as well as a pencil, simply will not be verified; it will not work. And that is all that 'working' means. Let's try another illustration, this time from Sidney Hook: * I start to drink some water and detect a taste of bitter almonds. Perhaps the water is poisoned. How can I tell? There is no cat handy to try it on, so, heroically if foolishly, I decide to test it myself. It may be that my last words are: 'Oh yes, the water is poisoned!' Nevertheless, the consequences are satisfactory in terms of the experiment—although that may be the only thing satisfactory about it. But since Dewey is so often held for believing that *anything* which satisfies him is true, he ought to be allowed to testify for himself:

Since William James has referred to me as saying 'truth is what gives satisfaction,' I may remark . . . that I have never identified any satisfaction with the truth of an idea, save *that* satisfaction which arises when the idea as working hypothesis or tentative method is applied to prior existences in such a way as to fulfil what it intends. (4:320)

The only desire that enters, according to my view, is desire to resolve as honestly and impartially as possible the problem involved in the situation. *'Satisfaction' is satisfaction of the conditions prescribed by the problem.* Personal satisfaction may enter in as it arises when any job is well done according to the requirements of the job itself; but it does not enter in any way into the

* In his *John Dewey*, John Day, New York, 1939, p. 76.

determination of validity, because, on the contrary, it is conditioned by that determination. (19:572; italics added.)

The determination of truth, then, is not a matter of feeling. It depends upon a theory of knowledge and of ideas, and follows as a matter of course once the functional or experimental approach is accepted. This may well mean that Dewey is simply by-passing the whole classic 'problem' of truth. Certainly he tried to by-pass the folk-talk of truth. In 1938, when his *Logic* was published, Dewey was finally prepared to reject the term 'truth' from his philosophic vocabulary (he also at this time rejected 'pragmatism,' at least as a noun). His substitute, 'warranted assertibility,' is not calculated to excite anyone. Yet it does try to describe what goes on and to that degree is an effort at candor. What goes on would seem to suggest that truth is a class name applying to a series of truth-ings, that instead of being a noun or a substantive, 'truth' should be regarded as adverbial or adjectival, and would be a more accurate symbol if we could always translate it into 'truly' or 'trueed,' and that it is plural rather than singular.

It may be pointed out parenthetically that in the present-day Oxford school of linguistic analysis, there are some indications that this whole approach to meaning and truth may be catching on—although it is only fair to say that, if this is so, it would seem to represent an independent movement, and that, in any case, no indebtedness to American pragmatism can be looked for. But the idea, now popular in British philosophy, that meaning itself is a matter of function and use, and that truth must be interpreted in a 'verificationist' way, as well as the steady attack on mind-body dualism—these are unquestionably congenial to Dewey's thought. However, it may be too much to expect that his pioneer work, like Peirce's, will come to be appreciated in transatlantic circles.

In conclusion, we may observe that Dewey's interpretation appears to gainsay what Truth 'ought' to mean—something monolithic, already there, or at least a replica of what is already there. (How these alleged qualities of the true would apply, for instance, to an invention or to the report of a man being saved from drowning is, Dewey confesses, a mystery.) This fixed and honorific designation of truth is not only a matter of vocabulary; it is the result of a decision to commemorate rather than to analyze a dominating human activity. For this reason Dewey's analysis may never satisfy a certain kind of temperament. To ask for the meaning of the true, the beautiful, or the good is felt to demean them and to indicate an irreverent attitude. For this reason also it is not easy to appraise the instrumentalist theory of truth. It is a theory, to repeat, of a special kind of *meaning*. If from one side it appears to debase the value of truth, from the other side it will seem a truism; from one point of view the whole enterprise is rejected, from another it will be seen as trivial. This may be inevitable when the search has to do with meaning.

To return to the figure used at the beginning of the chapter, let us look at, if not through, that second lens of man's bifocal vision. This epistemological lens produces the traditional problem of knowledge, which is the problem of knower versus the known. How can the contents of the mind, images and ideas, be related to the actual objects for which they stand? How can we get out of our heads to compare what is in our heads with what is not? This is the *general* problem of knowledge, the problem of whether we can know anything at all. (That there are *specific* problems of knowledge—indeed, without a problem there is no knowledge—is basic to Dewey's exposition.) Such an *überhaupt* problem is rejected by Dewey on at least two grounds. The first is its guaranteed insolubility, since, as stated, the problem precludes an answer. Secondly, it assumes that experience is suspect, which is clearly untenable since any epistemological analysis must start with, rely on, and return to that very experience. Were we to follow traditional philosophic usage in examining, say, the phenomenon of ingestion (this is Dewey's example), we should first make a clear-cut separation between food and the eater, turning them into two different dimensions. Right away there would be a towering problem of getting them together again. In time a school of eaterism would emerge and, of course, a contrasting school of foodism, and philosophy would go on its merry way. It is as if a physiologist, for the purpose of studying respiration, isolated the air, the lungs, or something more detailed. Then, after he completes his analysis, he finds that cooperation of air and lungs has become a total mystery and is probably impossible. These illustrations will seem caricatures because we are not prepared to break into two metaphysical realms the transactions of ingestion and respiration. But knowing is also a transaction, an insoluble problem arising only when it is arbitrarily broken into two or more unjoinable parts.

We have had occasion to refer to 'transaction' before. Dewey and Bentley have this to say about it: 'Our own procedure is the *transactional*, in which is asserted the right to see together, extensionally and durationally, much that is talked about conventionally as if it were composed of irreconcilable separates.' (18:69) 'Irreconcilable separates' are very often the result of what, as we have seen, Dewey calls *the* philosophic fallacy, which is the reading back into an antecedent nature the results of philosophic analysis. For example, if it is analytically necessary, as it may be, to isolate knowledge from the knower, sense data from what we actually do experience, lungs from the air, stomach from food, very well. But if these procedural distinctions, made for a specific purpose, are now installed into a prior world, if what comes last in analysis is made first in existence, then inquiry is blocked and meaningless problems are institutionalized. The transactional approach is designed to correct the fragmentation of experience, on whatever level it may occur.

But even if knowing is a genuine transaction between different aspects of a natural world of events, in what way are these aspects related, between what parties does a transaction take place? It may seem that Dewey's approach is intramural only, confining itself to human interests and problems; that when it addresses itself to ideas and their verification it never appears to break the circle of inquiry and reach out to a nonhuman and metascientific order; and that there has been altogether too much attention paid by him to 'experience' and too little to realizing that 'the world and truth are the bright goals of free men,' to quote a contemporary existentialist. Maybe the identity theory has been put aside too cavalierly. Even if it has not, the question implied—what is the object of knowledge, to what does it point?—is still one that has not yet been adequately handled.

Inquiry, Knowing, and Truth

Dewey is, of course, a realist, believing that there are objects unaffected by knowing; if not, knowing would be mere pretense. But he also believes that *what things are like before inquiry is undertaken is indeed the specific business of the inquiries themselves,* and it would be meaningless to raise the question outside the context of such inquiries. This is, in part, the implication of a transactional point of view. And it must raise questions like these: What happens when inquiry takes place? What is the status of the product of inquiry? What is the meaning of the antecedent reality that knowing both assumes and discloses? These questions will plunge us immediately into deep waters.

Let us take as an example of antecedent reality what is sufficiently remote from human manipulation and experiment, a star in the sky. By 'star in the sky' I do not mean merely the speck of light seen on a moonless and cloudless night or reflected on the photographic plate of a telescope, but rather the physical object itself, the incandescent mass. Admittedly, what I seem to be talking about is itself an inference based on, among other things, specks of light, the science of astronomy, and so on—but let's not arrest the analysis at the beginning on grounds of first-degree epistemology! If one were to exclude the 'actual' physical star from the matrix of inquiry in favor of 'mere' sense data like lights in the sky, if one were not to accept 'reality' as what knowing is about, then inquiry simply becomes senseless. Contrariwise, if one were to assume that the star is, as it were, *just* a star, with no way of eliciting a response in me, then there would be nothing at all to talk about, no problem, not even anything to be called a star. The whole business would be of as little concern to me as it now is to a paramecium. As a matter of fact, neither one of these extremes is ever taken seriously, at least outside the precincts of professional philosophy. What both science and enlightened common sense have settled for is really a transaction—whatever it be called—in which there is a constant to-and-fro process between different *temporal* phases of a total act of knowing.

In his *Logic*, Dewey suggested a possible terminology for this ongoing activity. (14:105ff) It may seem a little forbidding but, if attended to, should prove of help. He calls the first temporal phase of knowing the 'subject-matter.' This refers to the original *non-cognitive* situation. Should we say this is the physical star itself plus its surroundings we shall be talking proleptically, for 'physical star' is, of course, what is going to emerge from the inquiry and will be called by Dewey the 'object of knowledge.' It would be more accurate to say that 'subject-matter' stands for the antecedent state leading to inquiry. We must remember that experience, for Dewey, can be pre-cognitive and non-cognitive. Discourse is not exhaustive. This is an important point because, as we have already noted, it is not the standard philosophical position. Dewey insists that knowledge occurs within the context of that which is not knowledge, i.e. directly experienced subject-matter such as lights reaching us from the evening sky. Unless these sensations provide a stimulus for asking questions, we shall know no more about stars than does the dog baying at the heavens. This does not mean that there is an unknowable and inaccessible subject-matter cut off from us in some Kantian fashion. It is rather that 'when the situation in which such material exists [man-looking-at-sky-and-beginning-to-wonder] becomes problematic, it provides precisely that which is *to be* known by being inquired into.'

The intermediate stage of the knowing process Dewey calls the 'content' of knowledge. This refers to subject-matter undergoing inquiry, in which one passes from various levels of indeterminacy through tentative and provisional decision to a terminal judgment about the 'object of knowledge.' The procession of man's first wonderings about the starry heavens above to the development of astrophysics would be an illustration of the 'content' of knowledge; and the star as we understand it now, or shall understand it better in the future, is the 'object of knowledge.' During the process of inquiry, it may well be that necessity and convention compel giving one phase the name of another, but what Dewey is underlining in his terminology is that *if we don't distinguish the 'object of knowledge' from something else there is no meaning to inquiry*. Ordinarily we use 'object of knowledge' indiscriminately, including both the antecedent stimulus to inquiry and the result of inquiry. Dewey prefers the phrase to be restricted to the latter, whereas 'subject-matter' or, possibly, 'physical object' should be reserved for the former.

The problem that this terminology is directed to is: Just what, if anything, is changed by the process of inquiry? Well, what is changed, or at least rearranged, is, first of all, the original problematic situation giving rise to the whole affair. But, in effecting such a change, an entire series of overt activities may have to be initiated which, as in the present case, may redirect the very course of intellectual history. A lot has to happen before a 'star' can come about. In this particular instance, the problematic situation could have been simply a primitive wonder at the twinkling lights in the sky, or a doubt that they were really gods, or a more sophisticated query as to whether all heavenly objects were the same. In resolving or changing that situation of doubt, a star, as the case may be, emerges as the object of knowledge. To be sure, 'something' had to have been there; if not, one is again led to ask why there was any difficulty in the first place.

But should it be insisted that what is discovered—the star—was there all the time and that really nothing at all has been changed except the mind and knowledge of the observer, then it has certainly been forgotten that 'star' is already an object of knowledge resulting from a whole history of inquiries extending over thousands of years, and that we are now reading it back as an independent physical object without noticing how such an object of knowledge developed from an undetermined subject-matter. In the course of that inquiry many things have happened—light has been captured and analyzed, instruments invented and perfected, mathematical computations made and new calculi devised, expeditions equipped and sent forth, not to mention overpowering cultural changes—all in a non-experimental science like astronomy with its aloof subject-matter. To say that *nothing* has happened in the course of the inquiry except in the mind of the questioner, and that the final object of knowledge is in no way to be distinguished from something else (i.e. 'that which is *to be* known by being inquired into') is to push the spectator theory so far that it makes knowledge simply inexplicable.

To try another brief example: An unidentified airplane appears in a sector being observed by a civil defense watcher. Now, planes are not always something-to-be-identified. They may be ignored, wondered at, empathized with, and so on. That there is *something* which is the subject of these and other reactions—even if only a cloud formation or the distorted position of a bird—no one would ever question. If there were not, then the reactions would be quite unaccountable. In the present context of a plane observer, the flying object becomes something-to-be-identified in terms of its nationality, destination, type, and the rest. The flying-object subject-matter begins to acquire a certain function as it appears in this particular context, as it becomes part of this transaction. It becomes 'known' then as such-and-such an object, with these or those specifications. Should we switch to the pilot flying overhead, we should also be switching our context. The plane to him, as he is now flying it, is quite different from what it is to the observer, even though they should agree on certain common ways of describing it. The terrain he is passing over may or may not need to be identified, and the same is the case with the rooftop on which the observer is stationed. Should the situation change and object-on-the-ground become, in turn, something-necessary-to-be-identified, then the watcher himself acquires a new place in still another transaction. To say that, as a result, nothing whatever happens in this plane-and-observer transaction as the result of these goings-on is to take a quite Pickwickian view of the realities of an air age.

The present exposition will have failed its purpose if it has not thrown some light on Dewey's view of knowledge as a relating process. What has been argued is that some parts of experience are connected with other parts, the indeterminate and less fixed with the settled and established. If a statement like this should still have a subjectivistic flavor, to the effect that Dewey must believe we can never get out of our heads to break the circle of inquiry, the exposition will also have failed; for the point of the preceding argument has been to suggest the *temporal* and *functional* rôles played by symbols like 'antecedent reality' and 'object of knowledge.' They emerge and have offices to perform as problems are raised and met. Foundational for this argument is, of course, the Deweyan interpretation of experience and continuity outlined earlier. It cannot be repeated too often that experience is not a veil coming between man and nature, that it is a relation between organism and environment which is itself natural and existential, that what is experienced is not simply more experience but a natural and real world. At the same time it must be understood that man cannot know what he doesn't inquire into, that a forever unknown and unknowable reality is just that, and that calling 'the world and truth the bright goals of free men' must mean—if anything at all—the giving of value to the stimuli and purposes of human inquiry. Dewey's contribution here—the idea of the solidarity of experience with nature and of knowledge with search—is crucial, not only for grasping a man's philosophy but for understanding the whole temper of a scientific age.

5. Thinking, Logic, and Scientific Method

If 'experience' is the key signature to Dewey's philosophy, 'thinking' is the very melody itself. There is nothing in Dewey, said Justice Holmes, but some variation on the theme of 'how we think.' Yet even here the stereotypes continue to distort, so that there are those—and they include professional philosophers—who hold that Dewey 'degrades' thinking by making it only 'a scheming and a planning.' Further, Dewey's emphasis on thinking, whether in general philosophy or in education, is seen by some as an overemphasis upon the intellectual part of man's make-up at the sacrifice of the emotional and appreciative factors, while at the same time others see him as the prince of anti-intellectualism. Glaring discrepancies like these are not necessarily contrived ones, even if they tend to cancel each other. They seem more like reactions to a truly revolutionary force and exemplify the difficulty of fitting Dewey's logic into already prepared preconceptions.

These preconceptions seem to oscillate between the notion that thinking is so much the exclusive property of mind that it somehow drops out of nature altogether, and the contrasting belief that logic mirrors the very structure of things. But in either case the act of thinking makes no difference to or in the natural world. Thinking is certified in various ways, but rarely does the certification depend upon what actually happens as the result of the thinking process. On this point the traditional empiricist joins the rationalist. Thinking involves logic, not behavior. And as such, according to Dewey, it becomes a complete mystery.

Before this point can be developed we must first recognize that the term 'thinking' carries an almost insupportable weight. It has become a symbol for almost anything that goes on in our heads—imagination, memory, belief as opposed to knowledge, guessing as well as understanding: 'thinking' acts almost as a synonym for consciousness. There is nothing we cannot think of and, as Dewey has observed, if we offer a penny for your thoughts we don't expect to strike a great bargain. It is clear then that 'thinking' needs to be restricted. Not that there is anything wrong with autistic thinking—that for its own sake. If we did not dream in the light we would be cabbages. In fact, reverie (when innocent and inoperative) would be close to the immediate or 'having' dimension of experience, the degree of closeness depending on the development of the experience from a truncated one to something full and consummatory. But if there is to be analysis, some discriminations need to be made; a familiar one is that which sets off reflective or critical thinking as a noteworthy and characteristic form of human activity quite different from imaginative fantasy or customary uncritical thought.

The question, then, is why thinking becomes reflective or critical. Why is not all our conscious life confined to daydreaming or to following habit patterns? They are certainly less trouble. We don't have to be urged to them as we do to critical thinking. That is assumed to be hard work, even unpleasant. The assumption that thinking is onerous (from now on, 'thinking' used by itself will mean reflective or critical thinking) may suggest that we think only when we have to, that we are forced out of habitual and dreamlike routine by—well, by a problem. Certainly by now this is to be expected. Dewey's argument here, as in knowledge, truth, value, and almost anything else, is genetic and historical. The origin and also the directive purpose of thinking are what concern him, for without initial impetus and aimed-at goal, thinking would be without meaning.

Almost anything can act as a motivator of thinking. Whatever sets us to doubting what up to then had been taken for granted is a potential stimulus. It does not have to be 'practical' except in the sense of effecting, or trying to effect, a solution to a problem. Of course, a problematic situation will not automatically coerce us to think. Doubts can be resolved by flipping a coin or by listening to habit. The opportunity to think can always be passed over. But it is not easily passed over when there is a genuine problem. What, then, is a genuine problem?

Dewey's example of the forked-road situation, in his little *How We Think* (1910), has become something of a classic. Simple and homely, it nevertheless contains all the elements of a genuine problem. We walk along a path and come to a fork in it: which turning should we take? Were there no branching of the path, we should continue on our way, pleasantly daydreaming or perhaps thinking critically about something unconnected with the walk. Or, if ours was an aimless stroll and we did not care where we went, the fork would not present a problem; we could go either way as fancy directed, or even retrace our steps. To make the forked-road situation the setting for a genuine problem and therefore the stimulus to thought, however rudimentary, there must be what William James called a real, live option. That is to say, the alternatives to decision must be incompatible—we cannot do both, not, in any event, at the same time; and we must be motivated to select one of them. Such a situation puts a premium upon reflective activity.

The person trying to get home or out of the woods before dark finds that situation in the forking of the path. To be sure, he still would not *have* to think. He might simply keep to the right (being an American) or he might toss a coin. But the more real and the more alive the option, the less likely he would be to follow habit or impulse. He would undoubtedly review his knowledge or woodlore, scant as it might be; try to anticipate the outcome of taking this forking or that; and calculate the chances of reaching his goal, using whatever information he could gather. This would be a reflective use of experience.

But reflective problem solving goes beyond experience. We must keep in mind that experience is a transaction and that *both* environment and organism are implicated in it; problems are connected with nature just as they are with experience. Therefore the problematic situation, like all transaction, is two-way. There must be a conscious agent, to be sure, if thinking is to take place; but the conditions preceding inquiry and inaugurating it, not to mention what happens as the result of inquiry, are also a part of the total situation. This is why, as has been noted before, Dewey can refer to the situation itself as problematic or indeterminate,* for the conditions leading to thinking are, he says, those of 'imbalance and disequilibration that recur rhythmically in the interactivity of organism and environment.'

* There have been some changes in Dewey's vocabulary on this point. For one thing, he has tended to talk more about an *indeterminate* situation than a *problematic* one, thus emphasizing the situation itself as a basis for thinking. On the other hand, he finally came to distinguish *doubtful* from *indeterminate*. 'Doubtful' assumes the interposition of an inquirer, whereas at one time Dewey seemed to be saying that a situation itself could be doubtful. (*Cf.* 17:327.) In any event, Dewey is trying to understand doubt as something more than subcutaneous behavior and different from mere

Within the transaction of experience there are ruptures and blockings as well as continuity: this is what drives men to think and animals to respond ingeniously, and also makes possible the relevance of thinking and intelligent behavior. For example, food is not always forthcoming when the tissue changes of hunger are operating. Were nature never to provide what can be used as food, there would be no life; were food always present without ado, there would be no problem. Characteristically, the hunger-food situation does present a problem that is not insoluble. This is why there is learning and, ultimately, with other situations, thinking. And this is why learning and inquiry are neither gratuitous nor ineffectual. The situation itself provokes the activity which reflexively will (or may) change it.

We left our discussion of reflective thinking at its point of origin, the forked road. In his *Logic* (1938)—the subtitle of which is 'The Theory of Inquiry'—Dewey returns to the same question but with many changes in terminology, some of which have just been noted. Perhaps the most important is his substitution of 'inquiry' for 'reflective thinking.' The term was originally used by Peirce to represent the activity directed to overcoming a state of doubt. Dewey's dissatisfaction with 'thinking' was, of course, part

---

pretense. ('Let us not pretend to doubt in philosophy what we do not doubt in our hearts,' said Peirce in his criticism of Descartes.) H. S. Thayer in *The Logic of Pragmatism*, Humanities Press, New York, 1952, has made a critical but not unsympathetic study of this point along with others. He finds that the terms Dewey employs to describe the problematic or indeterminate situation seem to break into two classes, those which have a *physical* referent and those which are of a *behavioral* nature. Thayer adds that this is a linguistic distinction and does not entail anything like a mind-body dualism.

of his whole rejection of knowing as the exclusively mental reactions of an idle spectator. 'Inquiry' seems to connote something more active and operational than does 'thinking.' It is a term broad enough to include all that goes on in the transformations instituted to solve a problem. For Dewey, inquiry is 'the controlled or directed transformation of an indeterminate situation into one that is so determinate in its constituent distinctions and relations as to convert the elements of the original situation into a unified whole.' (14:104–5)

A definition like this for a key term in a book on logic will provoke an entire constellation of questions clustering particularly around the word 'transformation.' The questions are much more than terminological ones. It is not so much whether 'inquiry' or 'thinking' is the more felicitous symbol as it is whether transformation-of-a-situation has anything at all to do with logic. The point is crucial. Dewey's basic presupposition, here as elsewhere, is a naturalistic one: inquiry (thinking), like knowing and valuation, is to be regarded as the natural activity of a human organism living in a precarious world. It is grounded in the very make-up of the organism, in the ongoing behavior of active agents dealing with a not yet completely determined environment. There is, as Dewey calls it, a biological matrix for inquiry, a continuum stretching back to the very adjustments that help to define protoplasm itself. (Since man is a social animal, there will also be a public and cultural matrix for inquiry.) Any other assumption makes problem-solving operations like knowing and inquiring miraculous interventions, non-natural and superfluous, falling somehow outside the orbit of evolutionary change and so outside the realm of the explainable.

Dewey is arguing that changes are indeed effected by inquiry; things happen and get done; situations are, to some degree, transformed; transactions do take place. He points out that, first of all, the source of inquiry is an existential situation, fluid and changing, 'so that in any case *something* different is going to happen in the future'; next, just what will happen depends on the introduction of other existential activities; finally, as a result, the original situation is so modified that, at least in some cases and to some degree, its indeterminateness is removed. Dewey gives a number of illustrations of this process. Take one of them:

> . . . that of a person who, being ill, deliberates about the proper course to adopt in order to effect recovery. (1) Bodily changes are already going on which in any case will have *some* existential issue. (2) It is possible to introduce new conditions that will be factors in deciding the issue—the question for deliberation being whether they should be introduced and, if so, which ones and how. (3) Deliberation convinces the one who is ill that he should see a physician. A proposition to this effect is equivalent to the conclusion that the consequences of the visit are calculated to introduce the interacting factors which will yield a desired issue. (4) Hence, the proposition when executed actually introduces intervening conditions which interact with antecedent existing conditions to modify their course and thus influence the issue. The latter is different from what it would have been if inquiry and judgment had not intervened—even if recovery of health is not attained. (14:163.)

What is unique in this kind of analysis will appear if we put alongside it the traditional interpretation: 'The propositions "I am ill" and "When one is ill, one should consult a doctor" are taken respectively as the minor and major premises of a syllogism from which the conclusion "I should see a doctor" necessarily follows.' This standard account, Dewey goes on to say, means either (a) judgments to this effect have already been made in the past and the present propositions are only linguistic records of former genuine inquiries; or (b) there is no problem, since when ill one summons a physician unthinkingly as with a reflex or conditioned response. In either case, nothing is explained. Dewey believes his interpretation at least explains the effective nature of inquiry. This effectiveness is not defined in terms of personal interest; the homeliness of the example could be replaced by the most 'impractical' of speculations without changing the point at issue. This point is that inquiry is more than an internal change of mind; it entails a change in the problematic *situation* that generates inquiry. Inquiry makes a difference. If not, it wouldn't be inquiry.

It would be tedious to repeat that inquiry (reflective thinking) does not exhaust human experience, that there is autistic thinking, that immediate and non-cognitive consciousness extends beyond the range of critical reflection—and that these activities are maximized not minimized by a valid philosophy. It would be equally tedious to describe again the transactional elements constituting a situation, or to insist that in any act of inquiry what results is different from what started the process, just as directly-had-but-not-yet-known experience is different from what comes to be known, known as the outcome of a process. What therefore is unique in Dewey's approach is that *inquiry is experimental.* Before we develop this and so connect inquiry with scientific method, let us first follow Dewey in analyzing inquiry into its various stages.

In both *How We Think* and the *Logic,* he identifies a number of steps (five in one case, six in the other) in the complete act of reflective thinking or inquiry; the two sets differ in some respects. In neither case, however, is the analysis simply an exercise in taxonomy; it is rather an attempt to see just what is essential as inquiry proceeds from the pre-reflective to the post-reflective. But there is no suggestion that some established routine must be traced in thinking or that one stage has to follow another in order at a fixed interval. In simple cases of problem-solving there might be just a single undivided act, although even here analysis would probably be able to isolate several functioning elements in the act.

The first step is not really part of the process at all, since it refers to conditions antecedent to inquiry, those of the indeterminate situation. To call this situation problematic is actually to advance a step, for it is only when it is subjected to inquiry that the original indeterminacy acquires the form and focus to allow intelligent handling. To be sure, the original situation—say, a general feeling of malaise—must have a pattern sufficient to constitute a situation; otherwise, as Dewey says, it would simply be indeterminateness-at-large, which might provoke nothing but blind panic. The second step, then, is that of setting up a problem which can at least indicate a solution. It is a preliminary diagnosis, however unpolished. In the present case, the malaise may come to be seen as illness and not some passing discomfort. Possible suggestions for meeting the problem can now appear. This third step, were it to function in the context of scientific inquiry, would be that of hypothesis, although the term might be inappropriate in the present common-sense instance. In any event, some ideas—i.e. plans of action—for handling the presumed illness must emerge, if not here then at some other early point. Some tentative sources of action must be available if inquiry is to continue. These suggestions will ordinarily be based on the previous experience of the inquirer, but there is nothing in the analysis which would preclude suggestions arising from intuition or any other creative source. In the case at hand these suggestions might be to the effect of simply remaining in bed until the feeling passes over; or of getting up and forgetting, if possible, the whole thing; or of trying out some patent remedies from the medicine chest; or of calling a physician. When these possibilities are present, then, as a fourth step, deductions can be made from them. This is the if-then stage, one of reasoning in the narrower sense of the word. What implications will follow if any one of these suggestions is put into operation, what is entailed by calling a physician or by remaining in bed, what further meanings are involved? On the basis of developing such further meanings and of anticipating what consequences may ensue, a choice is made among the available suggestions.

In *How We Think*, Dewey recognizes the resulting fifth step, that of verification. In the *Logic* this becomes 'the operational character of facts-meanings.' But in both statements the same point is made. It is that a consistent dualism between ideas and facts would effectively prohibit any possibility of verification. There would be no way of bridging the gap between hypotheses considered as purely ideational and consequences regarded as only factual, unless it be 'recognized that both observed facts and entertained ideas are operational.' 'Operational' here refers not only to Dewey's earlier contention that ideas are indeed plans of action and thus *possible* operations; it now should be added that facts—at least as they function in the field of inquiry—are by no means autonomous. They are selected and described for a particular purpose, that of the inquiry itself. In that context facts *become* evidential just as ideas ask for evidence.

What Dewey is attempting in this kind of analysis is not merely an essay in classification. (In the *Logic,* he adds a sixth aspect in which he compares common sense with scientific inquiry.) Its purpose is to propose that inquiry represents a fusion of elements which ordinarily have been regarded as joined only in some special or contrived sense. Not only idea and fact are seen to be functionally related, but induction and deduction in general, not to mention the beginning and close of inquiry and thus past and future themselves. These appear in Dewey's analysis as operating parts of a single act of problem solving, each part relating constitutively to another, just as in the knowing-known transaction. So far as the time element is concerned, recognition of these stages would indicate that inquiry is a developing and growing process, whether short or long, that novelties and transformations do play a determining part, and that investigations start, change, and stop. In short, the distinctions that emerge in the process of inquiry are not to be read back into it as if they were there petrified from the very beginning. They are rather to be understood prospectively as steps to be used in the growing course of a particular event. It is largely for this reason that Dewey chooses to identify them. The analysis might also suggest that the routine of inquiry could apply to any problematic situation, from that of common sense through the technicalities of scientific method, and, at least theoretically, to those fields which are still regarded as outside the range of intelligent understanding and control, chiefly the field of value.

What has all this to do with logic? The answer has been, characteristically, nothing! Logic is an independent and self-enclosed system of relationships cut off from, but not cut out of, other forms of experience, having its own canons and its own autonomous life, if not, indeed, its own mystique. Dewey's approach, it is alleged almost tediously, may have something to do with psychology, education, sociology, possibly scientific method; but his *Logic* has little if any logic in it. In fact for some of the critics it is a scandal. The logician is not always sure whether what he himself legitimately studies actually mirrors the structure of things, the reflection being caught in an immediate intuition, or whether it is merely an interesting system of self-revealing tautologies. In any case, it is something quite different from problem solving, from biological or cultural contexts, or even from the experimental procedures of scientific inquiry. On this point, for once, there is little misunderstanding of Dewey. Yet there seems to be as little appreciation of the re-evaluation he is proposing, a re-evaluation which Sidney Hook suggests may prove to be Dewey's principal contribution to philosophy.

In considering that contribution we can start by accepting without hesitation the unique quality of the syntax of logic, just as we can of mathematics. We can also accept, as does Dewey himself, the autonomous nature of logic in the sense that it is independent of metaphysical and epistemological presuppositions. In some important sense it does have a life of his own. But this life of logic is not therefore a mystery or unfathered. It arises in the course of inquiry and is dependent upon it, just as laws arise in the course of and depend upon the relations of man to man in society. *The* Law—whether it be common, Roman, or something else—may finally achieve the independent status that goes with the name, but it is fatal to forget that the autonomy of symbol-systems is an achievement and not an antecedent reality. All such systems, even the most august, must be understood in terms of the functions they perform.

The function of logic, for Dewey, is to formulate and generalize the conditions without which inquiry cannot operate. It is to determine the procedural rules that alone can make possible controlled investigation, just as it is the function of the rules of a game to make possible that control of activity which constitutes a game as opposed to unorganized play. This may be a misleading example, not because it is trivial but because it may be thought that the rules of any game are purely arbitrary—say, in baseball the runner goes to first base, to his right. Yet were one to investigate the history of the game, he might discover this procedure to be not entirely arbitrary but to be dependent upon the fundamental conditions of handedness, running, batting, and throwing. Be that as it may, the binding rules of baseball—although subject to change—have consistency and independence, majestic enough when pronounced with authority by a masked arbiter, yet they are hardly outside experience.

'All logical forms,' Dewey insists, 'arise within the operation of inquiry and are concerned with control of inquiry, so that it may yield warranted assertions.' This means 'that the forms *originate* in operations of inquiry.' (14:4) As always, Dewey is looking at origins. It is here he finds the 'justification' of logic, rather than in its impeccable syntax. Logical rules make possible the very routine of inquiry; without them there can be only unorganized improvisation and problems solved merely by accident. But these rules are not therefore imposed upon the materials of inquiry from without; they have grown up in the course of inquiry, as have the rules of arithmetic in dealing with countable and measurable material, taxonomic systems in dealing with the investigation of organisms, the law in dealing with social behavior. Thus, Dewey's logic—as Ernest Nagel has said of it—is 'the morphology of inquiry.' It needs to be studied in its natural habitat, which is not necessarily that of the textbook. The textbook is restricted almost exclusively to proof, the very essence of logical operation, but proof itself arises in the process of reflection: it is the test of the effectiveness of inquiry, the cement that holds 'if' and 'then' together.

Consider what is without doubt the unique characteristic of at least deductive logic, the ability to achieve necessary and compelling conclusions. There is nothing mysterious about it. The processes by which one proposition follows rigorously and inexorably from another are conditions or stipulations which make thinking possible; without them the operations by which we should try to progress from one stage of inquiry to another would become meaningless. Certainly four is the sum of two and two, and John Smith must be mortal if he is human and if all humans are mortal, because if these conclusions did not follow there would be no intelligible syntax to arithmetic or to language. Nothing would be said. Four *is* a two and a plus sign and another two. This is what, among other things the symbol *4* means. There is no independent law above human experience which makes deductive entailment function the way it does. Nor is its validity established exclusively by a routine of logic entirely cut off from its results. Were the results consistently mischievous or unintelligible and kept telling us, for instance, that John Smith was immortal and that $2+2=4.3$, then the 'extra superfine' quality of deduction would turn into a caricature. It is of enormous importance to have, as in mathematics and general deduction, logical relationships which are coercive and exact. But these relationships cannot be divorced from their origin and context. That context is always procedural—the procedures used by the human animal in trying to solve its problems. 'If-then' is one of such procedures, an extraordinarily exciting one, to be sure, but not immaculate.

Furthermore, the 'if' should provide insurance against the absolutism of the 'then,' because the first principles of even deductive logic are by no means the pure deliverances that, say, the axioms of Euclid were once thought to be. These first principles must be regarded as postulates, as a form of hypothesis, the value of which depends upon fruitful consequences. The relation between the non-Euclidean geometries of the nineteenth century and the doctrine of relativity in the early twentieth century is one of the most elegant specimens of the way unusual postulates (in this case, about parallel lines) can lead to the richest of results. This is in no way a denigration of first principles; it is simply that they need to conform to the requirements of any sound hypothesis—that predictable consequence can flow from them. Their 'iffy' form indicates this.

In the closing chapter of his *Logic* and elsewhere, Dewey

makes a compelling point in showing that although there has been great advance in logic, such as in the development of probability calculus and symbolic form, there has been little interest in relating the canons of logic to scientific inquiry. Instead, the tradition has been one of selecting a single phase of inquiry—especially connected with an antecedent theory of knowledge—and making it exhaustive. He traces examples of this from the history of logic. Now, it may be that the term 'logic' should not be used for what Dewey has in mind, just as it may be argued that 'truth' cannot adequately be represented by 'warranted assertibility.' Dewey recognized this. At ninety, a year in which he seemed to have made a number of vocabulary adjustments, he wrote that 'the force of the word "Logic", in all probability, has overshadowed for the reader the importance of what in my intention was the significant expression, *The Theory of Inquiry*. For that misapprehension I accept full responsibility.'* But whether or not 'logic' and 'inquiry' are synonyms, the point Dewey is making is a crucial one and it seems to be this:

Logical and non-logical behavior have been separated by philosophic tradition decisively and existentially, whereas Dewey regards the first as developing out of the second. He believes that the logical derives from the alogical, that logical form accrues to activity when the activity is that of inquiry, that subject-matter acquires a certain kind of pattern when it comes under investigation. There is for him no contradiction between these forms of behavior, any more than there is between random finger movements and those articulated into the performance of a piano sonata.

* *Journal of Philosophy*, May 6, 1949, p. 341.

Nor is one kind of activity merely a potential or implicit expression of another kind of (logical) activity; finger movements are not merely an unfulfilled sonata. The argument is simply that when non-logical or pre-logical experience runs into trouble, it needs to be transformed so that what has proven ambiguous or problematic may be rectified and continuity restored. In the course of restoring continuity—the goal of inquiry—certain techniques become generalized and organized so that they can be available for future use. Dewey holds this to be the genesis of logical forms, forms which therefore are neither miraculous nor trivially tautologous but which run along on all fours with other activities.

There is a spread of such organizing forms. They may range from the quite simple models of systematic common sense, such as thing, cause, purpose, to the most stringent procedures of scientific experiment, from everyday deductions to the most rigorous of mathematical analyses. But in each case the forms of inquiry, according to Dewey, have arisen from the problem-solving activities of men and derive their function as they contribute to the forwarding of such activities. After all, men did investigate before logic was perfected. As John Locke put it, man did not have to wait for Aristotle in order to become rational. The structures of inquiry develop in the course of inquiry, which suggests that the methods of human thinking have changed (or ought to have changed where they have not) as have the conditions men have faced. As with all the arts, techniques of control arise within the ambit of the material being worked upon, not outside it. Failure to recognize this has been one of the great human tragedies—this at least is Dewey's contention. For such failure has led to the belief, on the one hand, that all inquiry must be patterned on a single model, perhaps that of physics; while, on the other hand, there is the belief that certain areas of human experience, such as values, are forever opaque to inquiry. The present argument is that all areas of experience are equally real and have their own unique problems and therefore their own unique modes of solution. This is not to say that there are no common problems or common techniques crossing between them. It is to say that no single pattern of investigation is exhaustive and also that no single field of experience is without any pattern of investigation.

The name 'experimentalism' has been given to Dewey's logic. Not because he was himself a great experimenter. He was not, except, of course, in the field of education. Moreover, it has been noted by even sympathetic critics that Dewey was not exactly *au courant* in the matter of the latest experimental work in physical science—a fact he was the first to admit. But 'experiment' is a wide-reaching term, not confined to the routine of the laboratory or to the apparatus of technology, vital as they are. 'Experimental' carries above all the connotation of active and controlled knowing; in the same way it suggests a logic in which human thinking does make a difference, in which there is an authentic reconstruction of experience. Dewey's entire philosophy has been an attempt to apply such an attitude to every area of experience.

It has just been suggested that the experimental attitude is not necessarily a matter of gadgets and laboratory routine, of chromium, rheostats, and winking bulbs. There are, for example, valid experimental procedures in the biological and social sciences which can be conducted without electronic signals. What experimentalism signifies is a general orientation, one of expecting hypotheses of any nature in any field to carry with them the conditions for their justification or rejection. These operating conditions are not the monopoly of physics or chemistry. They may involve something as different from a cyclotron as the calling of a general election, or instituting a public health service based on the interpretation of vital statistics, or trying out new teaching devices, or investigating cultural value patterns through techniques of interview and questionnaire. But even if each area of experience demands its own procedures, yet the over-all tool is the operational spirit, which expects concepts to achieve meaning and validation by way of the institution of working programs.

Similarly, 'science' is not exhausted by the mathematical equation any more than it is by the *physical* experiment. Respectable scientific generalizations—say, those in physiology—can be established through ordinary language. This is in no way to minimize what is undoubtedly the chief operational tool of science, but it is to suggest that mathematical symbolism is no more fitted to serve as a model for all segments of knowledge than was Newtonian mechanics. Indeed, the collapse of the glorious eighteenth-century Age of Reason was in no small part a result of just this kind of disenchantment—disenchantment with the idea that all human experience must resemble the Newtonian cosmic machinery, a clean, deductive structure based on a few simple mathematical laws.

Equally inadequate is the notion that science connotes universal predictability and therefore a mystique of infallibility. Such a misconception falsifies what is, in fact, the heart of scientific method—the very institutionalizing of tentativeness and probable error.

At this point, however, the dangers of talking cavalierly about scientific method must be fittingly recognized. It is indeed too easy to talk about science, as they said of Francis Bacon, like a Lord High Chancellor. Philosophers need to be reminded that scientists themselves are quite wary about referring to 'scientific method' *in general.* It has even been argued that an appreciation of science can best be brought about through a study of the history of great experiments; here it will be seen that perhaps no two crucial experiments ever used the same 'scientific method,' that many of them outrageously violated the most respectable canons, and that the personalities of the scientists themselves had a great deal to do with the nature of their experiments. This may be too extreme a position, yet it is a healthy reminder that 'scientific method' is more than a high-order abstraction.

Despite this reminder it is inevitable that some general notion of the nature of science will emerge, especially if, as with Dewey, a key philosophical problem is the possible applicability of science to a field such as that of human values. There are, of course, many such general notions, and even to inventory them would be a formidable task. One of the most orthodox descriptions is that science is an attempt to secure, in a given area of human experience, knowledge, prediction, and control of sufficiently general a nature that they can be applied to a number of particular cases. When, in 1950, the Ford Foundation decided that human behavior was indeed a proper matter for intelligent inquiry, it laid down a number of suggestions (requirements, really) as to what such inquiry entailed. Those requirements included such things as: formulation of general concepts and deductions from them; refinement and constant testing of such theoretical formulations; research designed to operate with carefully selected variables and to relate in a significant way various social science disciplines; repetition of studies; and so on. Exacting as were these criteria, a number of research projects on human behavior already published have apparently lived up to them.

But the point is not to multiply approved descriptions of scientific method, much less to propose unorthodox ones. It is instead to indicate those scientific attitudes that seem to have been responsible for the impact of science on the modern world of ideas and that promise the possibility of extension to fields of human experience other than the ones already exploited by science.

One of those attitudes is the operational or experimental temper, which has already been discussed here at length. Another is suggested by the continuum stretching between so-called common sense and even the most rigorous of the sciences. This continuity of inquiry has impressed all the American pragmatists. Peirce called an essential part of his own philosophy 'critical common-sensism.' William James distinguished between common sense, science, and philosophy, but felt each was appropriate in its own field and as to which was the truer, 'God only knows.' Dewey's exposition of the steps of reflective thinking is an analysis which tries to make clear the easy transition from lay intelligence to scientific.

A third attitude is the indispensable spirit of tentativeness and hypothesis. To be scientific is not merely to use instruments. Much more significant than any particular scientific routine or technique is the use of the tools of probability, critical caution, and what Peirce called 'fallibilism.'

These are the only weapons which can overcome the suasion of allegedly final judgments and of dogma, and they may constitute the unique contribution science can make to modern culture. This is not a matter of sweetness and light or even of the liberal temper. It is simply that were science as inflexible and absolutistic as some other human enterprises (examples of them depending on one's personal bias), it could never accommodate itself to the dramatic changes of a world in process. And were man to remain as unaccommodating as sometimes he seems determined to do, he would find himself with the dinosaur.

In Peirce's emphasis on the self-corrective nature of the scientific task, in James's almost poetic open-mindedness and abhorrence of the dogmatic, in Dewey's constant stress on the problematic and the hypothetical, American pragmatism has been all but the trumpet of the new learning (to use Bacon's phrase). But it is not that this is merely a philosophy celebrating something it possibly doesn't understand very well; rather it is a philosophy urging that scientific *attitudes* such as these be extended to all sections of man's life. All human experience that makes a claim to *knowledge* needs the cool touch. It is to this fundamental aspect of Dewey's philosophy that we now turn.

6. Values and Inquiry

More than once in the preceding pages it has been said that for Dewey every area of experience is equally real, that no particular logic or experiment can serve as the model for all inquiry, but that no field of experience is automatically excluded from some kind of reflective and critical investigation. These contentions apply particularly to the general field of value, and even to mention them touches off a predictable and well-nigh universal reaction, almost as familiar in science as it is in philosophy. It is a reaction that can be documented by volumes of quotation, all to this effect: Values are normative and facts descriptive, and there is no way of bridging the gap. No argument can advance logically from a premise with only an 'is' to a conclusion with an 'ought.' Values are either subjective, emotive, matters of wish and arbitrary choice and so can never be handled objectively and rationally; or they are absolute and nonempirical deliverances and therefore just as unamenable to secular inquiry. Between logic and morals, between man's control of the world and of himself, between what men know and what they do, has arisen an implacable dualism.

This familiar veto—already something of a cliché—upon the rôle of intelligence in ethics can be rephrased in a number of ways. In the most general terms it proposes to stand as an injunction against any misguided attempt to reduce ethics to something else, say, to biology or social psychology. In more specialized language (as in the so-called naturalistic fallacy), the veto is to the effect that the 'good' itself cannot be reduced further, any more than the experience of the color yellow can be reduced to wave-lengths, for they are something else. Bishop Butler's remark that 'Everything is what it is, and not another thing' has become a most fashionable maxim in ethical theory. It may well be, as was noted earlier, that the good is as indefinable as is yellow, or, what amounts to the same thing, that it rests on an intuition of fittingness or something like it. In any case, the attempt to handle values as other things are handled is held to be at least irrelevant.

If this is not serious enough, still another block to inquiry about value will be encountered. Even should one be driven to acknowledge that *x* is valuable and good, he can then go on to ask: 'But why am I *obliged* to do the good? Granted that something like Dewey's idea of total integrated experience is somehow a source of value, why *ought* I strive for it?' (The name for an area of questions like these about duty and obligation—distinguishing as they do between the right and the good—is deontology; and some recent thinkers are even prepared to raise the question 'whether we ought to do what we ought to do.')

How can we respond to questions like these? Can they be answered or must they simply be by-passed? It may be that Dewey's frank admission (if that is the correct word) that the quality of an experienced situation is immediate and incommunicable goes part way in meeting at least the questions about the indefinability of the good; but even if it does, it certainly will not take us very far toward reaching an intelligent approach to valuation. To advance along this path and, at the same time, to take account of the classic dualism that has given rise to questions like the foregoing, we must avoid being compromised in advance. We are in danger of being so compromised by the very statement of the fact-value problem. The problem—like the mind-body 'problem'—is really a covert definition, or possibly an assumption, which begs the question at the very start. Fact and value are presented as already so different that no significant commerce can take place between them. But this is the very proposition needing to be demonstrated. More than that, the cutting off of value from fact is also assumed to be established purely on a priori grounds. On the other hand we may have here simply one more example of the dualism bequeathed to us by a cultural heritage. It will be remembered that Dewey has tried to show that the very reality-appearance dichotomy itself and all the dislocations inherited from it have a natural history and must not be assumed to have been theoretically and finally established. At one time the orbit of science did not include the stars, or disease and insanity, or even the drifting of the clouds or the working of a pump. Some of these were indeed considered sacred and invested with what was thought to be an indestructible tabu against the ministrations of intelligence. It would be unkind to draw the parallel. A generation ago, in *The Quest for Certainty,* Dewey asked for another Copernican revolution which, among further changes, would remove from the center of thought the fixed idea that some regions of human experience must remain forever impenetrable to inquiry.

We are also compromised in advance if the enterprise of science is held to be morally neutral, having nothing whatsoever to do with values. This has no longer the strength it once had, but it still operates as an effective block. Its strength has been dissipated as scientists themselves have come to recognize the impossibility of an insulated science secure from atomic shock. It would be banal to trace the political and moral education of physicists in the last decade but, journalistic or not, the point is clear—an amoral scientist is not quite a full human being. But it is more than this, because scientists have also come to recognize the predominant part selection—therefore valuation of a sort—must play in their work. The analysis of the problem, the selection of variables, the experimental design are all dependent upon the choices of the scientist, so that, as Hadley Cantril shows, scientific 'objectivity' refers to the accepted rules of empirical research only *after* the above elements have been decided. In that decision, a number of executive scientific values play their part, like parsimony, elegance, fruitfulness, the insistence on communication and on public verification. To neglect these would be to remove much of scientific meaning.

To put it another way, the scientist is not impressed by just any old fact. Everything is not taken into account. Certain data are accepted, others are rejected, still more neglected. As with his choice of what he feels to be significant problems, so with the scientist's choice of significant data: more accurately, those data are significant that are selected. Indeed, instead of *data* (givens), one might substitute *capta* (takens). It is not too much to say that data (facts) are those objects and events which the scientist (not to mention the man in the street—overworked as he may be) has agreed to choose as important. The facts of chemistry are not the facts of the everyday world—acids and bases are factual for one, hard and soft for the other. But neither are the facts of everyday common sense entirely unselective: many allegedly non-factual things are omitted—dreams, hallucinations, ghosts, even neuroses.

They are omitted because, in an admittedly arbitrary manner, they are judged to be not entirely relevant, and need not be reckoned with as sticks and stones and rain have to be reckoned with. In a similar way, the facts of American history will probably not include your Aunt Minnie. But her facts, too, are limited and determined by what she must take into account as important to her. In this way the gap between facts and values begins to diminish. Facts themselves become a kind of value because of this act of preference, an act which effectively prevents the layman or the scientist from being completely neutral, much less indifferent.

The point must not be caricatured. It scarcely implies travesties such as that of the scientist loading his dice or preferring alkalies to acids because, for esthetic or political reasons, he doesn't want his litmus paper to turn red. If terms like 'objective' or 'critical' are appropriate to scientific method, as they surely are, their meaning goes beyond mere not-taking-for-granted or impatience-to-be-shown. They are not synonyms for indifference or neutrality, but, instead, turn upon the ability to select, to choose between alternatives, to say yes here and no there. And to choose is to establish or employ a set of values. Scientific objectivity is not equivalent to not-giving-a-damn. That it is equivalent to the discounting of personal prejudice is elementary and unexceptionable, but to take this as given should not reduce it to triviality. Objectivity becomes trivial when it becomes neuter.

It can also be argued that scientific method itself is one of the greatest of human values, a rather young and fresh one at that. It is a youngster of but four centuries or so, young as the middle class and the New World and the national states of Europe. The revolution which propelled it into life saw also the birth of the great trading cities and the rise of new theories of business and government, not to mention the rebirth of the humane arts themselves. Its method is throughout the product of historical processes, the end result of social decisions, some of them involving bare economic choices, others resting upon the most precious and intimate of human rationalizations, but all of them thoroughly infected with valuation. Natural science had to win its privileged position. It has been chosen as something important. Man has decided, at least in certain areas, to solve his problems through the use of intelligent control, free inquiry, and self-correcting instruments.

What Dewey is proposing is that eventually all problems must be so handled. But that position can be argued for on its own merits only if it be not vitiated at the outset by what may well be a series of dubious assumptions. That his own proposals are equally dubious, and that the definition of value presented earlier, of value as the outcome of a process of decision—and, thus, of possibly intelligent decision—begs at the very outset the question to be decided are also, of course, arguable points, and will be argued.

Let us start at a place where no real argument will be found. The one unexceptionable way in which values are clearly subject to scientific investigation is that of a thorough study of what men have indeed valued, an exhaustive inventory of the patterns of choices men have already made, and, where possible, a companion study of the reasons, at least hypothetical ones, for those choices. Few would quarrel with Dewey's own statement on this:

Values and Inquiry

Valuations exist in fact and are capable of empirical observation so that propositions about them are empirically verifiable. What individuals and groups hold dear or prize and the grounds upon which they prize them are capable, in principle, of ascertainment, no matter how great the practical difficulties in the way.*

Nearly all of contemporary cultural anthropology is devoted, at least in part, to this kind of material†; so is much of current sociology, not to mention clinical psychology. But, in general, philosophers have not been impressed.

They have not been impressed because, if purely descriptive, such studies are not part of philosophy; and, if they venture beyond description, the studies simply manifest the naturalistic fallacy. For what men do is no index of what they ought to do. Facts are descriptive only, whereas values are prescriptive. For instance, because the Kinsey reports show that most men and a sizable proportion of women have been, at times, unfaithful to their spouses does not mean that marital fidelity is any the less a virtue. After all,

* *Theory of Valuation,* monograph, op. cit. p. 58.

† Typical of this kind of research is the recently completed Ramah project, under the direction of Clyde Kluckhohn of Harvard, which is a detailed study of five intermingling cultures in an area of New Mexico, focusing upon value changes, or the absence of them, resulting from cross-cultural contacts. Other representative investigations have been directed lately to Hopi ethics, Navaho philosophy, Balinese religion, not to mention detailed clinical observation of the value patterns of American ex-urbanites and 'organization men.' These studies, which have enlisted the efforts of professional philosophers as well as of social scientists, have been aimed clearly at a descriptive study of 'what individuals and groups hold dear or prize and the grounds upon which they prize them.' The best bibliography of this kind of study is that of Ethel Albert, former editor of the Kluckhohn project, *A Selected Values Bibliography for the Comparative Study of Values,* Harvard University, 1954, mimeographed.

Saint Augustine knew much of what the Kinsey reports demonstrated. There just is no bridge between fact and value. We can always ask of a fact, even if it be a 100 per cent indefeasible one, whether it is good or not. Such, at least, is the general feeling of many philosophers.

The argument is a shrewd and somewhat teasing one, but there is less here than meets the eye. What does meet the eye squarely is the vividness of the contention that there are really two kinds of knowledge, or, more accurately, two kinds of question which can be asked. This insistence is almost a signature of much of contemporary philosophy. The kind of question so many present-day philosophers are interested in raising and trying to answer is one addressed to the *meaning* of the words used in ethics. To handle that area of question—say, about good, ought, right, moral intuition, moral sanction—careful analysis of language is what is required, and such analysis exhausts (or almost exhausts) the function of moral philosophy. The kind of question that is not of interest is the so-called naturalistic one, concerned with empirical knowledge about man and his society and the possible relation of such knowledge to human values. Inquiry of this nature, it is alleged, can have no bearing on the kind of question that characterizes genuine philosophy.*

* However, some recent books by philosophers may indicate something of a change in this attitude. See for example David Bidney, *Theoretical Anthropology*, Columbia University Press, New York, 1953; A. MacBeath, *Experiments in Living*, Macmillan, London, 1952; R. B. Brandt, *Hopi Ethics*, University of Chicago Press, Chicago, 1954; John Ladd, *The Structure of a Moral Code* (a discussion of Navaho ethics), Harvard University Press, Cambridge, 1957; Charles Morris, *Varieties of Human Value*, University of Chicago Press, Chicago, 1956; and also Ethel Albert, 'A Classification of Values,' *American Anthropologist*, April 1956, pp. 221–48.

Up to a point, this sort of argument is without exception. But the point is reached early, which is why the claim sounds more impressive than it really is. That a necessary function of philosophy is the analysis of meaning, and that this has been the case at least since Socrates, is not a matter of doubt. Moreover, an essential part of the accomplishment of John Dewey and of all American pragmatism has been precisely such analysis. We have already demonstrated, it is hoped, that it is the *meaning* of knowledge, truth, value, thinking, idea, and the rest that has been the focus of Dewey's attention. But—and this is the nerve of his argument—such meaning is more than a matter of verbal clarity or logical consistency, although it certainly includes them. The *meaning* of value is itself dependent on the process of human decision, of decision emerging from a problematic situation. This is the context of value. The context is one involving human needs, basic conflicts, societal adjustments, sometimes the very boundaries of sanity itself. To renounce that kind of vital situation in favor of exclusive concentration on semantic analysis would be, for Dewey, nothing less than the emasculation of meaning itself.

To put it less astringently, even at the risk of overworking still further a weary philosophic cliché, the kind of knowledge that has hypnotized much of contemporary philosophy is indeed a necessary condition for the discussion of value, but it is certainly not a sufficient one. Both analysis *and* descriptive knowlege are demanded, and as early as 1903 Dewey was asking that we look in these two directions if we wish to approach morality scientifically. One direction will consider all value statements 'with reference to their bearing or import in the determination of some further statement, *i.e.*, a consequent,' thus 'fixing [their] meaning (or significance) . . .' The other direction is empirical in its assumption that the 'basis and ground [of a statement about morals] lie outside of itself. This reference beyond itself sets us upon the search for prior assertions which are needed in order to make this one, *i.e.*, upon inquiry.'* It is the second direction which received more and more of Dewey's attention in the years following this early paper, and it presents of course the very point at issue in the whole controversy.

The point can be restated in the form of a question: Are propositions about values continuous with the rest of human experience? Dewey answers in the affirmative, the anti-naturalist in the negative. The naturalist, in other words, is not particularly interested in trying to 'save' value for philosophy by rescuing it from science. Increasing knowledge about human choices, about the psychophysiological needs and desires implicated in them and the cultural patterns determining them, knowledge arising from whole new areas in the expanding sciences of man—all this is to be welcomed, not deprecated. But it can be welcome only if the assumption of discontinuity be waived, the assumption that value-experience is not reconcilable with other experience. In *Human Nature and Conduct*, Dewey makes one of his significant attempts to explore the continuity expressed by the title. His theme may be found on page 12 of the Introduction: 'A morals based on study of human nature instead of upon disregard for it would find the facts

* This 1903 paper, which first appeared in the University of Chicago Decennial Publications of that year, is 'Logical Conditions of a Scientific Treatment of Morality.' It was reprinted in the volume *Problems of Men*, Philosophical Library, New York, 1946, pp. 211–49. The quotation above is from page 212.

of man continuous with those of the rest of nature and would thereby ally ethics with physics and biology. It would find the nature and activities of one person coterminous with those of other human beings, and therefore link ethics with the study of history, sociology, law and economics.' This is not the same point made earlier, to the effect that we can indeed learn more about the incidence of the valuation process and that there would be little exception taken to such an enterprise. It is now a matter of the continuity of *meaning*, the proposal here being that contributions of science represent more than a tidily classified inventory, that without such information we are confining the realm of value to a flat two-dimensional schema, all surface and no depth.

Take the familiar example of a qualitative experience such as that of seeing the color yellow. Now, to apply the celebrated maxim of Bishop Butler, this yellow color is what it is and not another thing. It must be appreciated 'phenomenologically,' which is to say without benefit of anything else, Angström units, for instance. Can there be any objection to this? Certainly not from John Dewey. We already have had occasion to develop in extended form his ideas of immediate consummation and qualitative incommunicability. No more than Locke or Berkeley would Dewey argue that one can discourse into a blind man the notion of color. What is forgotten by the critic of naturalism is that someone like Dewey has in mind a situation in which *there is a problem and therefore an attempt to gain knowledge*. It may be tedious to keep repeating this, yet it seems constantly necessary. The immediate enjoyment of yellow may be as phenomenological as you please. Indeed Dewey has not often been surpassed in his insistence on the inexpressibly unique character of such direct experience. But the distinctions he has made throughout, such as those between sense data and knowledge, unreflective and reflective thinking, bare enjoyments and values are distinctions addressed to the *meaning* of the latter terms—knowledge (better, knowings), reflective thinking, and values (better, valuings). The sheer appearance of sensations, unreflective thinking, and direct enjoyments—taken by themselves—does not necessarily involve a problem situation, and therefore it introduces no difficulty to acknowledge (nay, to insist) that these can be handled imaginatively and non-discursively in all their inexpugnable uniqueness. Thus, the color yellow can be relished in all its intrinsic singularity. Until it provokes a difficulty it has no meaning—no meaning, that is, as an item of value or knowledge. Dewey here is interested in *values* and *their* meaning, not in something else. To refuse to talk about *them* in descriptive and empirical terms, those of science, is at the same time to refuse to talk about the characteristically human problem-situation. This would appear to be an unreasonable restriction of interest.

In what is probably an unnecessarily bald statement, Dewey has this to say: 'The idea that *judgments* about valuings-values must themselves be made in terms of values is on a par with such views as that *judgments* of color must be settled in terms of colors, not of conditions set by vibratory processes or corpuscular shocks.'* Of course, as we have just been pointing out, in one important sense colors must be considered in terms of colors, even if that sense is not easily a matter of verbal discourse. It is the word *judgment*, which I have italicized in the quotation, that makes

* *Value: A Co-operative Inquiry*, Lepley, ed., Columbia University Press, New York, 1949, p. 76. Italics inserted.

Dewey's point. To limit the entire meaning of the color phenomenon to what is intuitively and directly grasped is, perversely, to put one's self in the position of being unable to answer some very significant questions about color—why some people can see it and others not, how it changes and how it can be controlled, what is the larger context of which this particular expression is a part; in other words, how color can be *understood.* Maybe the romantic idea that direct appreciation must always surpass understanding will exert a coercive power, until we realize that without understanding there is less chance of appreciation. We cannot always rely on luck.

Dewey's remark, however, may give the impression that color can be considered *only* in terms of 'vibratory processes or corpuscular shocks.' But surely this is not what was intended. The context of the statement makes quite clear (although it must be confessed that Dewey's words do not always make his point clear) that 'values' here connote the outcome of a problematic or judgmental situation rather than the immediate quality of an experience. In any case, both these dimensions are required to round out the field of value. What has disturbed Dewey and other naturalists is that one of these dimensions, that of analysis, has tended to pre-empt the philosophic concern in this area, forcing into alleged irrelevance the entire problem of the origin, context, functioning, and description of value, and therefore much of its meaning. This kind of problem demands the contributions of science. Without them, the anti-naturalistic rendering of value, however sophisticated the accent, must exploit the language of vitalism and literary psychology; and it must lead us to suspect that the invention of the naturalistic fallacy may be no more than an elaborate dialectical device designed to preserve an important segment of philosophy from the constant encroachments of science. The nakedness here seems to be almost as apparent as that of the Emperor under his imaginary clothes.

We have been speaking in general terms. Can anything more specific be said about the possible applicability of scientific method to values? In Chapters IX and X of *The Quest for Certainty*, 'The Supremacy of Method' and 'The Construction of Good,' Dewey presents one of his many attempts to reckon with this most perplexing of questions. He makes several suggestions. Basic to all of them is his contention that science is primarily method, although not a circumscribed or parochial method. 'The knowledge of the relations between changes which enable us to connect things as antecedents and consequences *is* science.' (9:274.) In his early 1903 paper, he had made about the same point: 'Scientific treatment of any subject means command of an apparatus which may be used to control the formation of judgments in all matters appertaining to that subject.' (17: 229.) To be scientific, then, is, among other things, to be able to judge what may follow from any given course of action. It is the organization of content so that knowledge of certain things depends upon knowledge of other things. The if-then step of hypothesis-plus-prediction is crucial and this step can be taken—with, of course, varying degrees of confidence—no matter what may be the subject involved.

In handling the phenomenon of valuation, this hypothetical approach is of overwhelming significance, for the process of choosing among conflicting wants and enjoyments—the process that, for Dewey, establishes values—is essentially a prospective one. It is a relation of what we are or have now, or have had in the past, to what we decide to be or have from this point on. To be sure, this procedure can be applied retroactively so that it becomes 'what we should have done,' but the point is no different—certain conditions depend upon other conditions, and the more we understand the conditions and their relationships, the more we can exercise decision and control. This, indeed, is what it means to be intelligent, should one balk at the term 'scientific.'

As a possible illustration of this if-then prospective aspect of the evaluation process, take the all-too-familiar problem nowadays of whether we *ought* to go on a diet of some kind—low-fat, cholesterol-free, salt-free, low-sugar. The problem is itself reducible to a conditional proposition and can be analyzed quite simply into an if-clause or protasis (if you want to be slim, maybe avoid coronary trouble and high blood pressure—and also not enjoy your meals) and a then-clause or apodosis (then you *should* refrain from eating this, that—everything). Now, the introduction of words like 'should' or 'ought' is expected, in much of contemporary philosophy, to have a paralyzing effect almost deliberately designed to arrest discussion. Yet such words have a clear enough function in a context such as the above; it is to connect judgments about a predictable and consequent state of affairs with those about an antecedent and conditional state. True enough, 'should' and 'ought' would seem to have a tendency to push back the consequences farther and farther, since we can always continue to ask questions like—why *should* I be slim? Healthy? Long-lived? Enjoy my food?—until to avoid an infinite regress one seems obliged to settle upon an ultimate 'ought' like happiness or duty, pleasure or benevolence. We have already suggested that most problems never reach this final barrier. But even if they did and forced us always into some absolute context, there still would be the two sets of judgments, one set resting upon the other, and the judgments would still be about *factual* situations—if I want to reach *Y*, then I *ought* first to secure *X*.

It is Dewey's contention that this kind of judgment (which, it will be remembered, he has called a judgment of practice) is a rather senseless one unless, like all means-end operations, it is based on knowledge, knowledge of the antecedents and knowledge of the consequences. In the illustration just used, a judgment about whether we ought to diet is at the same time a judgment about kinds of food, their relation to health, and the meaning of health itself, all of which depend on adequate information. True enough, the information may not now be adequate and may change as new research is forthcoming; our own experiment with diet may or may not be a convincing one. But any if-then, end-means proposition is literally meaningless unless there is knowledge about the ends which are wanted (and this holds whether they are ultimate or proximate ends), the means by which they can alone be reached, and the operational connection between the two. When such knowledge is reliable, organized, and of predictive significance we have science; its applicability to a *value* proposition would seem inevitable.

At this point it is only fair to notice that there is some evidence of a possible slowing down of the forces of intransigent anti-naturalism. A number of recent works in ethical theory have demonstrated a renewed interest in what may be called the possibilities of a science of ethics and definitely show signs that the purely emotive approach to values may be relaxing.* And in the general field of philosophy we are beginning to find talk of 'reunion in philosophy'† in which philosophic 'decision' is being asked for as well as exclusive concern with philosophic analysis. Professor White, for instance, suggests specifically a going beyond positivism and pragmatism and beyond the interminable debate of science versus ethics to a synthesis which will include, along with the analytic and antiseptic emphasis in contemporary philosophy, 'insight and the more humane, cultivated concerns,' largely esthetic and intuitive. Such a suggestion is not an isolated one, although it would be entirely premature to see a turn in the tide. Yet it may be that the 'defense of modern man' (in Charles Frankel's phrase) may again count on the philosopher as it has not been able to do for a number of years.

To return to the argument, what Dewey is saying is that the more we know, here as elsewhere, the less the number and the pressure of problems. Now this can be denied by denying two of his basic notions, one a definition, the other an assumption. The definition, it will be recalled, is that value is the result of a choice which involves some element of reflection or judgment. By its very definition, therefore, value must be observable and testable, and so potentially open to scientific treatment. To define value, on the other

* A most convenient summary of a number of such books can be found in Morris Keeton's extensive review, 'The Skeptic and the Rooster,' *Antioch Review,* XVI, 2, June 1956, pp. 243–56. See also the first chapter of Alexander Sesonske's *Value and Obligation,* University of California Press, Berkeley and Los Angeles, 1957.

† Compare *Toward Reunion in Philosophy* by Morton White, Harvard University Press, Cambridge, 1956. See also the concluding chapter in his *The Age of Analysis,* Mentor Books, New York, 1955.

hand, as immediate enjoyment, incommunicable and non-discursive, is to guarantee at the same time its exemption from any kind of knowledge. This matter of definition may underscore our earlier discussion of the difference between sheer enjoying and critical evaluation.*

The assumption which needs to be rejected in order to 'preserve' values from science is that values function in the context of human needs and desires. This kind of rejection is much more difficult to sustain than is the refusal to go along with Dewey's definition, since even when a negative or disvalue judgment is made about human needs and desires—as by the more dour forms of Christianity—even here information about what men like is imperative, so that those likes can be condemned. To regard value as discontinuous with all human experience except at such a meeting point as private intuition or a sense of oughtness (a kind of Cartesian pineal gland, where body and mind alone could meet) is not only to save values from science; it is also to turn over to private introspections, themselves notoriously discordant and dogmatic, this most characteristic item of human behavior. Surely the introversions of British dons and American professors, however suave they may be, are not to be considered philosophy's 'answer' to the growth of a science of man!

* On this point Dewey goes still further and argues that 'enjoyments that issue from conduct directed by insight into relations have a meaning and a validity due to the way in which they are experienced. Such enjoyments are not repented of; they generate no after-taste of bitterness. Even in the midst of direct enjoyment, there is a sense of validity, of authorization, which intensifies the enjoyment. There is solicitude for perpetuation of the *object* having value which is radically different from mere anxiety to perpetuate the *feeling* of enjoyment.' (9:267)

But we still shall be told that all this is not to the point. It will be granted that science can study values in an entirely descriptive manner; it may also be admitted that the expanding disciplines of depth psychology, social relations, cultural anthropology, and the like may indeed tell us more about man's needs and the ways in which they can be met—even the 'healthy' ways. But the point at issue is whether values can themselves be derived from or justified by scientific knowledge. It is this possibility that the critic of Dewey rejects, and it must be admitted that the rejection is forceful and not easy to meet. It is particularly effective because of its 'pragmatic' challenge, that is, its demand upon Dewey or his followers actually to make such a scientific derivation or justification of value. Or, in more technical language, the challenge is to reduce a proposition about the good to a proposition about something else. Because this kind of 'reduction' can never be found in an article, a book, or even in one man's entire philosophy, and because such reduction resembles a drill in logic less than it does a long-time cooperative venture in solving a scientific problem, the naturalist seems to be at a disadvantage and his position is regarded as weak. He is not always able to substitute facile feats of analysis for patient and sometime plodding research.

In a significant footnote (19:592), Dewey recognized that he himself had 'done little or nothing in the direction' of producing a technology which could relate intelligent action to such value-laden fields as politics, and in the closing pages of his monograph on valuation* he shows clearly that the application of science to values is still a promissory matter. The foundation may be in construction, but the edifice still has to be built. A futuristic approach

* *Encyclopaedia of Unified Science,* op. cit.

like this is always vulnerable. But having admitted this, the instrumentalist will suggest that nevertheless a start has been made in doing exactly what the anti-naturalist denies can be done and that these efforts will not forever be blocked—any more than those of sixteenth and seventeenth-century astronomy—by a pre-established and non-empirical logic. Many of these efforts were anticipated by Dewey and all of them fit into the theoretical framework he had prepared. The following suggestions are but a bare outline of what may well be the beginning of a new Copernican revolution in science.

To the number of assumptions we have been listing as basic for the Deweyan position one more can now be added: that there is no substitute for knowledge, not only when describing what men do but even in venturing to prescribe what they ought to do. Or, to put it negatively, ignorance is not the appropriate condition for making value judgments. This is not to assume that knowledge is tantamount to ethical theory—theory, even in science, is an independent variable. But it is to say that ethical theory, like all other theory, depends for its relevance upon knowledge and not, as has so often been the case, upon sheer charisma. Not that the two have to differ. Both Christian saint and tough-minded psychiatrist are in agreement when they insist that 'love is better than hate,' that 'one ought to love'; the saint, as well as the psychiatrist, may have based his judgment on what cannot be denied to be knowledge. But when a Karl Menninger, among others, demonstrates in detail the relation of mental health to the outgoing activities of what he does not hesitate to call love, and the contrary pathological tendencies involved in withdrawal and cruelty, experimental and verifiable knowledge about man and his interpersonal relation is, we feel, helping in some cases to justify, and in other cases actually to establish, norms of conduct.

Menninger* is but one of an ever increasing number of psychologists, psychiatrists, and social scientists who are coming to realize that among the functions of science is the necessity to throw as much light as possible on human options, not only as a matter of describing them but also in the hope of making a selection among them. Fifteen or twenty years ago this would have been rank heresy; it is no longer so. Men like Sullivan, Cantril, Fromm, Money-Kyrle, Parsons, Shils, Kardiner, Bronowski—and there are many others†—have been bold enough to include values as a

* The work referred to here is *Love Against Hate,* Harcourt, Brace, New York, 1942.

† Among the works referred to in this connection are the following: Kurt Goldstein, *Human Nature in the Light of Psychopathology,* Harvard University Press, Cambridge, 1940; Weston La Barre, *The Human Animal,* University of Chicago Press, Chicago, 1954; Abram Kardiner, *The Psychological Frontiers of Society,* Columbia University Press, New York, 1945; Karen Horney, *Neurosis and Human Growth,* Norton, New York, 1950; Erich Fromm, *Man for Himself,* Rinehart, New York, 1947; R. E. Money-Kyrle, *Psychoanalysis and Politics,* Duckworth, London, 1951; J. Bronowski, 'Science and Human Values,' *The Nation,* Vol. 183, No. 26, December 29, 1956; Hadley Cantril, *The Why of Man's Existence,* Macmillan, New York, 1950; H. S. Sullivan, *The Interpersonal Theory of Psychiatry,* Perry and Gawel, eds., Norton, New York, 1953; P. Mullahy, *A Study of Interpersonal Relations,* Hermitage, New York, 1949; Talcott Parsons and Edward A. Shils, *Toward a General Theory of Social Action,* Harvard University Press, Cambridge, 1951; Clyde Kluckhohn, 'Values and Value-Orientation in the Theory of Action,' (in Parsons and Shils, op. cit.). In this connection there also needs to be mentioned the new mathematical work being done in the calculus of human choices, an enterprise attracting the attention not only of economists and mathematicians but also of mathematically trained professional philosophers.

deliberate part of their work; and a number of them have been still bolder and have been prepared to propose that their study of human nature—both in its individual and cultural aspects, as well as in its conscious and unconscious—has led them to indicate the way human nature 'ought' to operate. Although there are inevitable differences in what they see as a healthy human nature, yet there is surprising agreement among them. Whether it be 'self-actualization,' 'positive freedom,' 'relief from tension and anxiety,' 'dynamism,' 'creative interchange,' 'human dignity,' 'total personality,' or something else (all of which are inadequately and almost caricaturishly denoted in a bare list like this and even by the bare labels themselves), the source of values appears to lie where Dewey located it: in an integrated experience where problems do not fester but are resolved.

Now, let us make no mistake. At this point the deontologist will again introduce his censorious and apparently devastating question: *ought* we solve problems, and *should* experience be integral? The anti-naturalist will continue to ask whether these things are truly good and, if so, how do we know it. Questions like these will still be supposed to serve as an impassable barrier. (Did not someone demonstrate that, on strictly aerodynamic principles, it is impossible for a bee to fly?) Yet scientists such as the above—and they will be seen to represent a cross-section of the highest respectability—have apparently been persuaded that the only result of this kind of interdict is to force us all into a blind alley. More than that, we can also point out that ought-questions have indeed been 'answered' in the history of philosophy and religion—God's will, conscience, duty, bare feeling, a moral sense, and many others have been solicited as sanctions, each with its particular afflatus. What is now being asked is simply that we look for the moral imperative in the nature of man. Unless the anti-naturalist is ready to separate values from any kind of manageable experience (and if he is, then argument must simply cease), this would at least seem a hypothesis to be entertained. Nor can it be put aside by asserting that the nature of man is no mystery, that it was as well known to Saint Augustine as to Sigmund Freud. New dimensions of man *are* being revealed; this is simply a fact which has to be taken into consideration. What is being asked now is that these new dimensions of the organic and social structure of man, unconscious as well as conscious, be enlisted in the quest for moral sanctions. It is not important at the moment whether these and other scientists are correct in the norms they are suggesting; it is important that they are daring to give us norms of any kind, based not on intuition or revelation but on meticulous clinical and experimental research. Here is an attempt to cut a Gordian knot.

Another knot is being loosened if not yet cut. Any scientific approach to value has been regularly tied up by what has been the fashionable doctrine of cultural relativity, the belief that 'custom is king' and that 'morals vary with geography.' There is nothing right or wrong in any culture that is not flatly reversed in another culture. Thus, any scientific study of value can be at most intracultural: one culture can never judge another. Without going into the details of this most controversial aspect of contemporary anthropology, it can nevertheless be said with confidence that the doctrine is not as modish as it was some decades ago, when Ruth Benedict's *Patterns of Culture* and the writings of Melville Herskovitz seemed to dominate the scene. Of course, one reason for the partial decline of the theory of cultural relativity was a political one, the spread of communism and fascism. When the murder of six million Jews and the liquidation of whole classes and nations were exempted from moral judgment by a doctrine like this, something seemed to be lacking. This is not to say that the theory is not still a powerful weapon, especially for the dislocation of prejudice; nor are we saying any more than that as an hypothesis it is simply not as popular as it once was.*

But it is more than politics that has cast doubt on the alleged impossibility of judging among cultures and on what Sidney Hook calls exaggerating the non-negotiable differences among men. More than thirty years ago, John Dewey was suggesting that there are forces making for moral stability:

> One is the psychological uniformity of human nature with respect to basic *needs* . . . In the second place, there are certain conditions which must be met in order that any form of human association may be maintained . . . In consequence of these two factors of comparative invariance, the extreme statements sometimes made about the relativity of morals cannot be maintained.†

This approach has been explored increasingly in the years since Dewey wrote, and although the question is still very

* A convenient summary of the present state of this problem can be found in a symposium of three articles in the *Journal of Philosophy*, November 10, 1955. Particularly helpful is the article by Clyde Kluckhohn, 'Cultural Relativity: *Sic et Non*,' pp. 663–77. See also the symposium 'The Roots of Value' in the *Antioch Review*, XVII, 4, Winter, 1957–58.

† From a chapter, 'Anthropology and Ethics,' in *The Social Sciences*, edited by Ogburn and Goldenweiser, Houghton Mifflin, Boston, 1927, pp. 34–5.

much a moot one, it would not be inaccurate to say that the hypothesis of pan-human needs and capacities serving to provide a broad outline for intercultural morality is being seriously entertained. That 'cultural differences are compatible with identity in value' is a thesis that is now being defended.* An interesting illustration of such possible value-identity is given by Clyde Kluckhohn † in which, among other things, he shows that no culture has accepted in-group suffering or cruelty as an end-in-itself, and that even the application of cruelty to the out-group is regarded as a matter of means, not of ends. Just so, no culture, not even that of the Soviet Union, with its official repudiation of immortality, has failed to memorialize death. Charles Morris, in the study we have already mentioned (*Varieties of Human Value*), has also been impressed by 'the orderliness and structure in the domain of value' and has gone so far as to identify some five common value dimensions that underlie cultural differentiations.

This is not the place to pursue the argument, exciting and significant as it is. The point has been introduced simply for two reasons. One is that the assumption of cultural relativity seems now less formidable as an interdict on any scientific attempt to handle value. The other is that, partially freed from the relativity veto, scientists have been searching for behavior traits that may indicate wide if not universal consensus. This is at the same time a search for the emergence of value-patterns and for their empirical sanctions.

* Cf. *Journal of Philosophy*, loc. cit.

† In *What is Science?*, edited by J. R. Newman, Simon and Schuster, New York, 1955, pp. 343–5.

The position here presented—which is Dewey's position—has of course been caricatured. Among other things, it has been labeled 'scientism,' a favorite whipping-boy term in some otherwise rather sophisticated books of recent years. 'Scientism' has been defined in many ways, most of them fulfilling the requirements of the straw man. It has been equated with 'historicism'—the attempt to turn what is into what is right. It has been regarded as the reduction of all science to mathematics. Above all, it has come to mean that nothing is exempt from the ministrations of science, and that whatever does not fit into its Procrustean bed is irrelevant or nonexistent. There may indeed be proponents of scientism as so defined, but if there are, Dewey is certainly not among them.

The point is so important that some recapitulation seems necessary. We have argued that scientific method is not exhausted by any simple technique, whether it be that of mathematics, history, or physics. Instead of being some kind of ritual, science is an attitude of approach and varies as does the subject-matter to which it is applied. Can it be applied to *all* subject-matter? Yes, to all *problematic* subject-matter, to all subject-matter that requires knowledge and judgment. That there is immediate and consummatory experience to which problem solving—and therefore science—is irrelevant, has been a prime insistence of Dewey. To interpret him, or anyone like him, to mean that non-scientific subject-matter is inconsequential or nonexistent is to conjure up for easy exorcism a masquerading ghost. Non-scientific subject-matter provides the brooding background, the matrix of human experience, parts of which are propelled to the foreground when there are ruptures or difficulties. To aver that science precludes 'wisdom' or 'art' or the 'preciousness of the individual' is, if honest, an unpardonably negligent misinterpretation of the attempt to apply science to values—'values,' for Dewey, being precisely those choices that are forced into the foreground of experience by some disturbance in the background.

Let us at least make the presumption that this is indeed Dewey's position. If it is a wrong one, what are the alternatives? If values are *not* amenable to intelligence and critical scrutiny, to what are they subject? Authority? Custom? Intuition? I don't mean that these sanctions collapse as soon as they are mentioned. But I do mean that there is nothing novel about them. So far as man's history can be traced, these have been forever the techniques of value establishment and enforcement. These have been tried and their success can be judged. Almost as if admitting this, the new best-selling anti-naturalists* have tried a bold new gambit, which is, in a word, that science has *already* been applied to values and look what has happened! We are now all 'predictable men' 'hiddenly persuaded,' 'organization men,' 'tomorrow (*1984*) is already here,' humanism is dead, Dewey has triumphed! Therefore, we must turn to something quite other than science; we must reemphasize what the sciences have all but plowed under. This may or may

* The following is just a bare sample of the books referred to here: Colin Wilson, *The Outsider*, Houghton Mifflin, Boston, 1956; and *Religion and the Rebel*, Houghton Mifflin, Boston, 1958; Friedrich von Hayek, *The Counter-Revolution of Science*, Allen and Unwin, London, 1952; Joseph Wood Krutch, *The Measure of Man*, Bobbs-Merrill, Indianapolis, 1954; Russell Davenport, *The Dignity of Man*, Harper, New York, 1955; Walter Lippmann, *Essays in the Public Philosophy*, Little, Brown, Boston, 1953; and at least the opening chapters of that otherwise delightful and provocative *The Organization Man*, by William H. Whyte, Simon and Schuster, New York, 1956. I am not including, of course, the work of professional anti-naturalists such as Reinhold Niebuhr and Jacques Maritain.

not be called 'religion,' but what man desperately needs today is not information about human conduct but something deeper, something unknowable and instinctive. Here is the source of value, and any attempt to analyze that source is at the same time an attempt to undermine the human dimension itself. Even democracy—unlike communism—must have its sanctions beyond this world.

The effrontery of an attack like this makes it seem slick—at least in a Madison Avenue way. The slickness rests on the switch that the sciences of man are already 'old stuff,' that depth psychology, interpersonal psychiatry, cultural anthropology, field approach to sociology and political behavior have had their day; and that what is really new in a bright shining package is good old-fashioned obscurantism. This is nothing less than the technique of the big lie: social science has been tried and found wanting and, what is worse, it is simply passé; 'religion' or some other more catchy symbol is the vogue and should now be given its chance.

That there have been egregious abuses of scientific method in such fields as educational testing, business administration, communication and advertising—not to mention other more respectable and academic areas—is undeniable; no less can it be denied that even Newtonian mechanics was abused when, in the eighteenth century, it was to command all forms of experience, even the incommunicable. Recognition of such evident gaucheries is one thing. It is quite another thing when in throwing out such dirty water, we also throw out the baby. Or, to change the figure without leaving the nursery, disciplines just getting started are to be smothered in their cradles before they can develop into maturity. Even this might be supportable if something were ready to take the place of the deceased. What, then, are the alternatives? Problems will be solved intelligently, or some other way. Dewey's entire argument stands on the premise that there is no substitute for authenticated knowledge *in dealing with problems,* wherever those problems may occur. Like Peirce, he pleads that we 'do not block the way of inquiry.' Is it this position that is somehow subversive—or is that term more appropriate for a mystique which turns away from the knowledge of good and evil, just as long ago Adam was turned away?

If Dewey's position is valid, it may be that the way to talk about values is indeed to talk about something else, Bishop Butler to the contrary notwithstanding. It has been said that a book on ethics need contain no ethical propositions. Although an exaggeration, the point is suggestive. What it suggests finally is that just as in the arts may be found the materials for appreciating the consummations of human experience, so in such fields as psychology, the sciences of behavior, and education may be found the materials for understanding the *problems* of human experience.

7. Nature, Communication, and Mind

In 1943, when the *Psychological Review* was celebrating its fiftieth anniversary, a survey conducted by the editors indicated that the most important article to have appeared in the journal up to that time was John Dewey's 'The Reflex Arc Concept,' which had been published in the third volume, July 4, 1896 (pp. 357-70). It must be remembered that psychology and philosophy had not yet been divorced in the nineteenth century; in fact, the academic marriage lasted well into the twentieth century. Dewey's studies were naturally in both fields and his earliest publications, books as well as papers, were devoted to psychology. It is no surprise, therefore, to find Dewey engaging in a technical discussion of what at the time seemed to be a dominating concept in the emerging young discipline of psychology, dominating because the way to make psychology truly a science would be discovered, it was believed, in the stimulus-response linkage and its evident relation to the cause-effect bond. It is something of a surprise, however, to find Dewey challenging the standard interpretation of the reflex arc and in terms which later would come to provide a familiar theme of his entire philosophy. The theme is that of 'transaction,' although the term, of course, was not yet a part of his vocabulary. It may be to some purpose, then, to review briefly his argument here as an introduction to a characteristically functional theory of consciousness.

Dewey's complaint with the reflex arc concept was that it seemed to imply 'a patchwork of disjointed parts, a mechanical conjunction of unallied processes,' (p. 358) whereas it should have been understood as a closed circuit in which each pole mutually affected the other. Radical as it may have seemed at the end of the nineteenth century, the reflex arc concept was simply not radical enough. There was a familiar dualism still embedded in the somewhat contrived relation between a physical stimulus and a psychological response. Instead of the coordinated solidarity and unity of an unfragmented whole, the reflex arc seemed to suggest a putting together of separated segments. Take the too familiar example of a child being burned by a candle flame (we had better make it a cigarette lighter). The reaction of the hand is not simply a 'response' to a light 'stimulus.' Movement is going on in any case; seeing-grasping is part of a larger coordination, and the response, says Dewey, is not simply *to* the stimulus but, as it were, *into* it. That is, the activity symbolized by the reflex arc theory is not that of a series of jerks, of something initiated at the push of a button. Such an interpretation (and Dewey was afraid it was the prevailing one) ignored the state of the organism prior to the stimulus, a state that was active, exploratory, already shifting and anticipatory before any stimulus was encountered. A sound, for instance, is not a solitary cause for hearing but is part of a total act, organic, not merely reflexive in character. Indeed, it is no paradox to say that responses are looking for stimuli, even for the 'right' stimuli.

What Dewey is arguing in this early paper is that the stimulus-response linkage must be understood organically rather than mechanically. This means that stimulus and response represent a redistribution of energies, as in the burning of a log. No particular aspect of the situation, say the striking of a match, can be taken as an independent and outside factor entirely cut off, as in this case, from the conditions which make combustion possible. Similarly a sensory stimulus—the flame of a candle—does not inhabit a separate dimension from that of the motor response—reaching, being burned, withdrawing. In fact, no 'mere' sensation or movement can by itself provide either a stimulus or a response; what is demanded is a total *act*, a reflex circle rather than an arc. Such an act may be discriminated into differently functioning parts for purpose of analysis, but, as Dewey will say later, to substitute the outcome of such analysis for antecedent conditions is to commit *the* philosophic fallacy.

Why are discriminations made within a simple act? Here Dewey again lays the foundation for later doctrine as he calls upon a problematic situation for an answer. When experience runs smoothly, there is no break between stimulus and response; the circuit is closed and there is no point even in separating the two. But when some difficulty interrupts the normal routine, special attention needs to be paid to different phases of a now problematic experience. Thus just as sense data *become* knowledge (or claims to knowledge) so the sensory stimulus itself is identified, discriminated, and separated from response when the occasion arises. Originating as it does in the context of a problematic situation, the distinction between stimulus and response should not then be installed as a prior before-and-after affair. The reflex arc concept seemed to do this, seemed actually to institutionalize a dualism between things and minds.

This résumé of an 1896 article is not presented for antiquarian reasons. Dewey's early argument is recalled because it illustrates what came to be the hallmark of his psychology—and not only of his psychology—and that is the constant attack on dualism. The attack here is going to be on the classic mind-body dualism, but, as we have seen in much of the previous discussion, this is only one of many alleged splits in the fabric of experience. For a while it became something of a cliché in philosophy to refer indulgently to Dewey's running battle with Descartes and others and to assume either that he was whipping a dead horse, or, more likely, overlooking a very live one. Such a reaction is no longer as fashionable as it once was. For one thing, the development of psychology and allied disciplines, including medicine, has increasingly emphasized the transactional and *gestalt* character of human experience and has tended more and more to put aside the traditional mind-in-a-body concept. In philosophy itself the familiar use of analytical procedures has had by and large the same effect. As an example, *The Concept of Mind*, a quite influential book by the distinguished British philosopher Gilbert Ryle (which, of course, makes no mention of Dewey) is devoted to an attack on the Cartesian 'ghost-in-the-machine' interpretation of the relation of mind to body, and proceeds to interpret consciousness largely in behavioral and action-centered terms. It may be that Dewey's work of a generation before will profit by the new vogue. In any case, we need to turn to his argument, which is not simply one more attack on dualism but is also a positive contribution to understanding the meaning of mind and consciousness, and to appreciating their continuity with the rest of nature.

The seriousness with which Dewey takes evolution has been noted many times. But here, in his attempt to fit mind into the world (which attempt, come to think of it, should never have been set up as a kind of labor of Hercules in the first place), 'the influence of Darwin on philosophy' becomes supreme. That influence is—or ought to be—in the direction of recognizing that a continuum stretches throughout the organic world and penetrates the inorganic as well. This recognition, among other things, is what it means to take evolution seriously. Among those other things is rejection of the assumption that, at least in the organic realm, objects or events are already so fixed in advance—as species were once supposed to have been—that change, if not impossible, is at least profoundly suspect. To take evolution seriously means also that origins and history are of capital concern: events are not rootless. Still another assumption—which may be an extension of the Darwinian premises—is the typical Deweyan insistence on process and context, the emphasizing of transaction instead of interaction between already established units. A constellation of evolutionary attitudes such as these has dominated Dewey's approach to experience, value, knowledge, thinking, and the rest; the same complex will lead to an exciting interpretation of mind as a distinctive mode of functioning rather than as a well-rehearsed actor awaiting his cue to appear on the stage.

Although Dewey does not have a developed philosophy of biology, this same approach can be applied to life itself and to the physical bases of life. Our interest here is in conscious life, but just as organic continuity does not break at some mark labeled 'nerve tissue,' so there is no complete hiatus at the point of the carbon atom and its chain-molecule manifestations. Inorganic nature itself demonstrates choices, closures, rejections; it may almost be regarded as ambivalent:

> Even atoms and molecules show a selective bias in their indifferences, affinities and repulsions when exposed to other events. With respect to some things they are hungry to the point of greediness; in the presence of others they are sluggish and cold . . . In a genuine although not psychic sense, natural beings exhibit preferences and centeredness. (7:208)

With Whitehead, Dewey is prepared to find an 'organismic' character in the physical world. Nature itself is a matter of transactions (Whitehead's 'feelings') and of resulting emergent *qualities*. It is an impoverished metaphysic which denies quality to natural events, and so must force into a supernatural region not only minds but values themselves.

What we call life seems to refer to those natural activities that are dominated by a need-satisfaction cycle leading to preservation and growth:

> Iron as such exhibits characteristics of bias or selective reactions, but it shows no bias in favor of remaining simple iron; it had just as soon, so to speak, become iron-oxide. It shows no tendency in its interaction with water to modify the interaction so that consequences will perpetuate the characteristics of pure iron. If it did, it would have the marks of a living body, and would be called an organism. Iron as a genuine constituent of an *organized* body acts so as to tend to maintain the type of activity of the organism to which is belongs. (7:254)

This interpretation is neither vitalistic nor mechanistic since it avoids both special forces and reductionism. As Dewey points out, vitalism (or, in other contexts, idealism) calls attention to the fact that earlier affairs prepare the way for later affairs, traditional mechanistic materialism to the fact that later occurrences could not have taken place without the earlier. Descriptively, both are correct. Metaphysically, neither is correct, since neither can be regarded as explanatory. What Dewey is urging is that there are 'plateaus' which exhibit different kinds of activity, levels at which emergent (a word he accepts with some hesitation) properties are manifested. But these levels are not breaks, any more than growth levels are interruptions of a continuous process. 'The reality *is* the growth-process itself.' How does mind fit into that process? To answer that, we need first to turn to language.

The fifth chapter of *Experience and Nature* opens with the homespun line: 'Of all affairs, communication is the most wonderful.' It is wonderful because it brings about a kind of transfiguration in which natural events leave the level of mere 'pushing and pulling,' mere physical bias and repulsion, and reveal themselves to man 'and thereby to themselves.' Communication signifies participation and sharing and is thus 'a wonder by the side of which transubstantiation pales.' Apostrophes like these may begin to indicate the place Dewey gives to *meaning*– for this is what communication brings about. Meaning is added to events, qualities cease to be dumb, understanding supplements appreciation, what once was simply a matter of 'having' is now transformed into what can be known, mind itself emerges–all at the touch of communication. In a more technical figure, communication–discourse and language–is the 'natural bridge that joins the gap between existence and essence.'

But this, it will be observed, is only lyrical. What is the

modus operandi of communication, does it have a natural history, and, above all, what are its relations to mind, i.e. which is cause and which is effect? In handling questions like these, Dewey uses the same analytical tool that is found in *Mind, Self and Society,* George Mead's epochal contribution to social psychology, although, strangely enough, there is no mention of Mead in *Experience and Nature.** It is necessary, even at the risk of over-simplification, to summarize Mead's position and see how the same pattern of explanation is found in Dewey.

To attempt to account for phenomena like mind, consciousness, and the self, one has to start somewhere. It is to no purpose, however, to start with mind or something like it, since this is precisely what is to be explained—not in descriptive or phenomenological terms (which are, of course, completely relevant in responding to another kind of problem) but in terms of origin. How did mind arise? What evolutionary force finally flamed into the lumines-

* It must be remembered, of course, that Mead's four books were all published posthumously, the first of them *The Philosophy of the Present,* edited by Arthur Murphy, appearing in 1932. *Mind, Self and Society,* edited by Charles Morris, was published two years later. So *Experience and Nature* antedated them by a number of years. Nevertheless, Mead and Dewey had worked together at the University of Chicago and Mead had published many early papers in which his own ideas had been expressed. In addition, Dewey had written highly laudatory papers on Mead's influence. It is simply strange that in Chapters V–VIII of *Experience and Nature,* where Dewey works out in greatest detail his theories of mind and consciousness, no reference is made to Mead. In passing, it may be observed with more than a little sadness that Mead's philosophy is apparently unknown to transatlantic thinkers and inexcusably neglected even by American philosophers. That neglect, however, does not extend to social psychologists and psychiatrists, many of whom, having rediscovered Mead, have made him the cornerstone of their interpersonal systems.

cence we acknowledge as consciousness? Putting it differently, what is the context or matrix of mind, the situation out of which the part is derived—or analyzed, as the case may be? For Mead's thesis is that the part cannot be explained without the whole. This organic whole, the basic ongoing event, he called the 'act.' The act is that complex of impulses which maintain the life process. It is fundamentally a transaction between the organism and the environment in which responses are made to selected stimuli. (Note the similarity here to Dewey's interpretation of the reflex arc.) It is also a transaction between organism and organism, so that the act is social, not 'merely' biophysical.

When organisms develop sufficient specialization—the development being in accordance with Darwinian principles—'the gesture' arises as the mechanism of the social act. Mead here relies on Wundt, the German psychologist, and also on Darwin. The gesture is the means whereby one animal makes the appropriate responses to another animal's behavior. Here is 'language' on an infraverbal level. The example of the conversation, even the ritual, of gestures between two strange dogs would be a familiar one. Now, it must be underscored that such language or communication is a matter of action, of behavior, not of the expression of an antecedent consciousness. Gestures are not even emotional expressions, as Darwin thought. They are part of the organization of the physical social act, functioning now as stimulus, now as response. (This may indeed be behaviorism, but it is *social* behaviorism. Like Dewey, Mead is quite critical of Watson's subcutaneous and individualistic behaviorism.) The level of the gesture is, then, that of the communication of *actions,* not of mental states.

For mental states to appear, in Mead's thesis, another

level has to be reached, the level of the *significant* gesture, or the symbol. This is reached when the gesture begins to point out a common object in the environment and to elicit a common response. More exactly, a gesture becomes symbolic and significant when it calls out in the agent the response that is being elicited from others. The gesture is then internalized. When, as in the animated cartoon, two dogs look knowingly at one another and make the appropriate reciprocal gestures when a cat comes in sight, and so prepare to act in concert, mind is born on the screen. Each animal begins to respond in the way it expects the other to respond and, despite Bobby Burns, to see itself as it is seen by the other. This is authentic language, whether vocal or subvocal, since communication now is assimilation, not merely transfer, of gesture. As in Mead's own example, when an animal can react not directly to footprints but vicariously to 'bear,' when signs turn into symbols, that animal has emerged to the level of mind. True, for this miracle to take place, many other things have had to happen, chiefly the growth and specialization of cortical tissue. Such growth and specialization are to be accounted for in the usual evolutionary terms, Mead argues, and not as mechanisms to express a substantive mind which somehow has been surreptitiously introduced along the way.

At this point Mead insists—and his insistence has been corroborated by the findings of neurology—that the patterns of the central nervous system are those of action, not of 'consciousness'; the 'act' is still the basic category, but not in a reductionistic sense. The 'act' is not an attempt to explain away. What it avoids—and this avoidance is itself a key to the meaning of scientific naturalism—is the introduction of special, rootless agencies to account for what needs to be accounted for. The emergent, irreducible phenomenon of mind, appearing at a certain stage of the communication continuum: this is what Mead has been attempting to trace. There is no occasion here to continue an exposition of Mead's argument, which proceeds to handle the development of the self, of rôle playing and the 'generalized other,' the distinction between the 'I' and the 'Me,' suggestions that have proved to be the very cornerstone of much of contemporary social psychology. Dewey, in a somewhat less technical fashion, continues along the same path of explanation.

Like Mead, Dewey starts with an ongoing vital process, in which gestures and cries are 'modes of organic behavior as much as are locomotion, seizing and crunching.' (7:175) Originally such gestures and cries were neither expressive nor even communicative, simply a form of instinctive motion. Under the pressure of circumstance, chiefly that of the social relations among organisms, certain of these instinctive sounds and motions—or, as Dewey puts it, their overflow—are captured in the net of use. This net is not yet the net of language, since language, for Dewey, depends upon symbols or significant gestures. It is simply that organic activities on a pre-linguistic level provide, as it were, the raw material of organized experience. Such activities, specifically sounds and gestures, like everything else come under the evolutionary pressures involved in survival and adjustment, in the course of which certain cries and motions are 'used within a context of mutual assistance and direction.' Some agreement in action, some sharing of experience becomes an imperative for a social animal: its survival demands communication whereby objects can become 'common' objects of meaning and hence of knowledge.

Before we turn to a further analysis of language, it is important to repeat that this attempt by Mead and Dewey to maintain, in their explanation, a biological continuity between language and what is not yet language cannot honestly be passed over as an example of the genetic or the naturalistic fallacy, any more than the theory of evolution itself can be. There is no attempt here to 'reduce' language, to make it nothing but something else, no attempt to deny the unique quality and function of symbols. On the contrary, it will be remembered that 'of all affairs communication is the most wonderful.' But language, even if autonomous, is not therefore autochthonous—which is simply to say that it did not spring out of the ground from dragons' teeth or, to change the myth, from the head of Jove. 'There is doubtless a great mystery as to why any such thing as being conscious should exist at all. But *if* consciousness exists at all, there is no mystery in its being connected with what it is connected with.' (6:62.) Consciousness, for Dewey, is connected with language, language with gestures: there is no break in the organic continuum. Neither is there a downgrading of any organic manifestation. 'The organism is a part of the natural world; its interactions with it are genuine additive phenomena.' (9:234.) It would be difficult to find a more convincing illustration of Dewey's anti-reductionist naturalism than these words from *Experience and Nature*: '. . . It is reasonable to believe that the most adequate definition of the basic traits of natural existence can be had only when its properties are most fully displayed—a condition which is met in the degree of the scope and intimacy of interactions realized.' (7:262)

If there is any fallacy operating in this tortuous area of mind and consciousness, it is more likely to be that which Dewey has dubbed *the* philosophic fallacy. It will be remembered that this is incurred when the results of analysis are set up in advance as antecedent entities. Nowhere is this kind of reification more flagrant than here. Indeed, Dewey feels that too many statements about mind and consciousness are only attenuated expressions of primitive animism. If this seems too harsh a judgment, perhaps the milder phrasing of someone like Gilbert Ryle may be appropriate: the Cartesian myth of the ghost-in-the-machine is 'a category-mistake.' When we regard mind as a separate substance entrapped, so to speak, in the body and somehow interacting with it, instead of as a symbol for a functioning process, we are simply looking in the wrong place and thus finding what is not there—or failing to find what is there. It is as if, in Ryle's example, a person were to be shown around Oxford and, after having had pointed out to him the various colleges, fields, walks, and even students, he were then to ask where the 'university' was. Mind is no more a separate entity than is the university—at least a separate entity in the sense in which the colleges are. It requires a different category, one of overall relationship and of the functioning of certain kinds of activity. Dewey and Mead, I believe, would agree.

Now, 'function' and 'functional' seem sometimes to be merely additional examples of currently approved words like 'dynamic,' 'process,' and the rest. Moreover, 'function' does mean a number of different things. What Dewey intends by the term and its cognates would seem, first, to be the straightforward sense in which they refer to the special or proper activity of anything—say, the function of the heart is to oxygenate and distribute the blood. Such a 'proper' activity inevitably implies purpose, and this, too, seems part of Dewey's use of the word. This is so despite his strictures against Aristotle. (In this connection it may be noted that Professor Randall has called Dewey the truest follower of Aristotle.) Still another connotation of function—at least in the present context—is that of the part or rôle played by anything, the transformation of activity under the pressure of circumstance. For instance, in an emergency, such as that resulting from a lobotomy, certain parts of the cortex can take over the activities of destroyed or injured tissue. In sum, an event comes to be functional when it performs or takes on an activity—usually a purposive activity—which otherwise would not have been effected. Still another sense of function is, of course, the mathematical, in which one quantity or measurement varies as does another. Although this is not directly connected with the present discussion, it may be used to return us to Dewey's analysis of communication, language, and mind, since it can be made to suggest that the independent variable here is the communicative process and not the mind. That is to say, mind arises and varies with communication and not the other way around.

Dewey, like Mead, has already tried to point out that language begins to appear when, because of the evolutionary need for shared experience, gestures become significant and, as symbols, call out similar responses and indicate common objects. When this kind of activity appears we are in the presence of mind:

> . . . 'Mind' is an added property assumed by a feeling creature, when it reaches that organized interaction with other living creatures which is language, communication . . . This state of things in which qualitatively different feelings are not just had but are significant of objective differences, is mind. (7:258)

An approach like this may seem unfamiliar to the point of paradox and so it requires elaboration even at the risk of repetition, for the present argument is of the utmost significance not only for Dewey's system but also for the whole course of contemporary thought, whether in psychology or philosophy.*

If the argument does seem to put the cart before the horse, it may be because our tradition, language, and even the syntax of our logic have conspired to present us with things instead of processes, substances rather than functions, the arrested not the flowing. This is why contemporary thinkers, far apart as they may be in other respects, have had to grapple with the problem of vocabulary. Philosophy of process (whether that of Whitehead, Bergson, or Dewey) seems to cut through the verbal categories of Indo-European languages at least.† Thus, the use of 'mind'

* In this connection it might be appropriate to quote what Morton White has to say about the influential contemporary thinker, Ludwig Wittgenstein: 'His interest in describing the role, job, and function of words is like the pragmatists'. His hostility to cartesian dualism and his preoccupation with shared social linguistic activity sound more like John Dewey than Dewey or Wittgenstein would have dreamed.' *The Age of Analysis,* Mentor Books, New York, p. 228.

† Studies of other linguistic systems, as Benjamin Whorf's work on the Hopi language, raise the interesting question of how much a particular philosophy rests upon a particular language. See, for example, Whorf's *Language, Thought, and Reality,* Massachusetts Institute of Technology, Cambridge, 1956.

as an antecedent entity, something which then is to be expressed via language, may be a prime example of an almost inevitable category-mistake and therefore largely responsible for giving Dewey's approach the air of paradox.

Mind, says Herbert Schneider, is 'simply nature feeling her way.' It *is* the meaning of events, the way they function when symbols have arisen, when therefore it is possible for one event to act as the representative or surrogate of another event. This begins to illustrate the difference between the functional and structural interpretations, since 'mind' is now being understood as the activity whereby one part of nature is able to indicate, signify, or simulate another part. (In more technical language, it is the activity that turns 'events' into 'objects,' since for Dewey, here close to Whitehead, 'objects are events *with* meanings.') Thus, 'ability to anticipate future consequences and to respond to them as stimuli to present behavior may well *define* what is meant by a mind or by "consciousness." . . . [Mind proves] to be a mode of natural existence in which objects undergo directed reconstitution.' *

* Dewey in *Creative Intelligence,* Henry Holt, New York, 1917, 39–40; and 7:220. Although in this passage Dewey seems to use 'mind' and 'consciousness' interchangeably, later on in *Experience and Nature* (pp. 303ff.) he distinguishes between them in terms of background and foreground or focus. That is, 'mind' represents the whole general system of meanings, whereas 'consciousness' is the centering of meaning in an idea. 'Mind is a constant luminosity; consciousness intermittent, a series of flashes of varying intensities.' (303) It will be recalled that, for Dewey, 'ideas' have to do with problem solving, and so 'consciousness, an idea, is that phase of a system of meanings which at a given time is undergoing redirection, transitive transformation . . . The *immediately* precarious, the point of greatest immediate need, defines the apex of consciousness, its intense or focal mode. And this is the point of *re*-direction, *re*-adaptation, *re*-organization.' (308, 312)

Nature, Communication, and Mind

In this whole discussion let us not forget the basic assumptions of an organic continuum and of evolutionary changes within that continuum, or, less abstractly, the basic idea that meanings are modes of natural interaction between organisms, which arise when problems of survival transform sounds and gestures into more complicated and specialized behavior. Putting it differently, new levels emerge within the general framework of nature, and on these new levels natural forces are themselves reconstituted. What is called 'mind' or 'consciousness' is 'the most wonderful' of such natural reconstitutions. But it would be less wonderful if such reconstitution of natural events were then read back into the process as a cause.

It is so easy here to commit *the* philosophic fallacy. Not to commit it, however, means to take naturalism seriously. To take naturalism seriously means, in turn, the avoidance of two extremes: that of inserting mind into nature in the role of a special and probably gratuitous god from the machine, and that of reducing mind to that which is not mind. To take naturalism seriously, in other words, is to realize that while mind is indeed part of physical nature it is at the same time dependent upon the specialized functioning of organisms. If a standard label is needed for this kind of approach, it can be called emergent realism or objective relativism.* That mind is 'real,' that 'it' emerges in relation to a nervous system and to certain forms of behavior, and still that it is not an antecedent substance forcing itself from without into expression—these positions

* This designation is used by Charles Morris, among others, in his *Six Theories of Mind* (University of Chicago Press, Chicago, 1932), which includes a most lucid exposition of the functional theory as presented by Mead and Dewey.

are all consistent with one another. For mind is neither an aberration nor a special creative power.

> Unless 'mind' was, in its existential occurrence, an organization *of* physiological or vital affairs and unless its functions developed out of the patterns of organic behavior, it would have no pertinency to nature, and nature would not be the appropriate scene of its inventions and plans, nor the subject-matter of its knowledge . . . Nothing but unfamiliarity stands in the way of thinking of both mind and matter as different characters of natural events, in which matter expresses their sequential order, and mind the order of their meanings in their logical connections and dependencies . . . That to which both mind and matter belong is the complex of events that constitute nature. This becomes a mysterious *tertium quid,* incapable of designation, only when mind and matter are taken to be static structures instead of functional characters. (7:286, 74–5.)

If this account is not what most of us ordinarily *mean* by 'mind' and 'consciousness,' Dewey would not have been surprised. What most of us ordinarily mean by these words, it may be conjectured, is a locus of sensations, qualities and values, a figurative repository of experiences which, although not easily described, are unique and entirely different from mindless and non-conscious behavior. But listen to Dewey: 'It is impossible to tell what immediate consciousness is—not because there is some mystery in or behind it, but for the same reason that we cannot tell just what sweet or red immediately is: it is something had, not communicated and known.' (7:307.) Thus, there is no quarrel here about the induplicable, qualitative feel of a conscious state; it is simply that it is not Dewey's purpose, as it would be, say, of the existentialist novelist or the depth psychologist, to *describe* what may very well be indescribable. It is his purpose to fit such possibly indescribable experience into a continuum of natural events and so, among other things, to insure against turning the indescribable into an explanatory substance. To say that mind and consciousness represent functions rather than things, relations not independent entities, that they offer a prime illustration of the transactional point of view—this is not to say that mind and consciousness are thereby exhausted without remainder and transformed into something else. As always, Dewey's interest is in origins and histories, in biology and evolution; this interest may prove a handicap for constructing a literary psychology, since the phenomenological analysis of conscious states will be conspicuously absent from Dewey's writings. But this lack (an esthetic lack if nothing else) is by no means tantamount to explaining consciousness away. Dewey's concern is *how* mind appeared in nature and *what* it does, but he was not a novelist.

In this whole discussion the term 'behaviorism' may still prove a block to appreciating a functional interpretation of mind. It is unfortunate that some of the exaggerated statements of the early Watson have tended to obscure the permanent changes in psychology resulting from behavioristic analysis, and it is also unfortunate that Watson's individualistic and laryngeal disposition of consciousness has yielded only with great difficulty to an interpersonal and intranatural treatment such as that of Mead and Dewey. But to say simply that their ideas can be labeled *social* behaviorism is very much of an understatement. What is involved in an approach like this is, as Dewey has put it, nothing less than the argument that 'social' is a category,* a category both of existence and of explanation. Relatedness is a basic trait of the world at all levels. Nothing in nature, Whitehead has argued, is simply and concretely where it is. While events do not belong exclusively to other events (which would be reductionism), neither are they exclusively solitary and singular. This relatedness becomes luminous as it appears on the level of communication between 'high-grade organisms,' yet the mind that thus emerges is nonetheless a social product. Indeed Dewey, like others, has been troubled by the use of 'I' as the sole carrier of experience, whereas 'it' might be more appropriate for indicating the participation that runs through all things. In any event, the self is not the source or author of consciousness nor its exclusive seat, which should be clear from the very phenomenon of language: selves are 'parties' and sharers, just as communication itself is the process of making common.

It was suggested a while back that this kind of interpretation may appear paradoxical. Yet it should be added that the interpretation is at the same time a familiar one, becoming more familiar as the transactional and interpersonal analysis of human behavior extends its jurisdiction. This is the reason why Gordon Allport,† for example, can say that Dewey is easily understood by American psychologists, for he was a pioneering exponent of psychology's 'fourth R'—relations. Just two examples may be selected out of many to indicate something of the spread of transactional psychology.

* On this point see Dewey's article in *The Monist,* Vol. 38, 1928, No. 2, pp. 161–77.

† In the *New Republic,* October 17, 1949.

Perhaps the most dramatic illustration is in psychiatry, where an identified 'interpersonal' school, making clear its indebtedness to Mead and Dewey, has played an increasingly important theoretical and clinical role. Harry Stack Sullivan, Patrick Mullahy, A. Kardiner would be among the leading figures, and the following exposition is largely from Sullivan's *The Interpersonal Theory of Psychiatry.* The basic assumption here is that mental disorder depends largely on inadequate communication, the result being anxiety. Each person, the argument continues, is part of a field rather than a separate entity, and his behavior and finally his mental health or disease are affected by whatever goes on in the field. When the dynamic flow of communication between various parts of the field is interrupted, what we call anxiety, mild or severe, results. This, it is claimed, provides an operational and transactional approach to mental disorder. Although, as with Freud, great reliance is placed on the early communication between parent and child, Sullivan finds the same difficulty with Freud that Mead and Dewey did with Watson, i.e. overemphasis of the subcutaneous. Behavior, normal or abnormal, is a function of the communication field.

Recent experiments in perception provide a second example of use of the transaction.These experiments* depend upon ingenious devices—revolving trapezoids, distorted rooms, slowly inflated balloons, and many others—which illustrate that a perceived object depends in great part

* The work has been done largely by Adelbert Ames, Jr., Hadley Cantril, W. H. Ittelson, and others. If the reader wishes a summary of the experiments, he can find them conveniently in Cantril's *The 'Why' of Human Experience*, Macmillan, New York, 1950, and in Kilpatrick *et al.*, *Human Behavior from a Transactional Point of View*, Office of Naval Research, Washington, D. C., 1953.

upon the 'set' of the perceiver and upon the successful or unsuccessful completion of the act which the perceiver makes to the deliberately manipulated stimulus. Going back to the reflex arc concept, it would appear that the experiments demonstrate convincingly that stimulus and response are not disparate elements somehow coming together in a fortuitous liaison, but that they represent analyzed elements of an organic fusion in which the conditioning and the expectation of the observer play a rôle no less significant than that of the intruding object. As Mead himself said, long before these experiments were devised, 'a perceptual thing is a combination of at least two characters, a distance character which leads to movement toward or away from it and the contact experience which results.' * This is a bare note on a significant contemporary research that has all kinds of promise.

Were it appropriate, many other aspects of transactional psychology and social science could be listed, such as the idea of rôle playing, the therapeutic use of psycho-drama, group dynamics, field hypothesis in political theory, the flash technique in esthetics, to go no further. True, some of these 'groupy' techniques have been abused to the point of caricature and may well merit the malicious travesties now being directed against them; nevertheless, a central theme seems now to have been established in modern psychology: that relationship is a dominating category and that mind may well be a dependent variable. The wider philosophical implications of an approach like this are impressive, for they seem to point toward a scientific and

* *The Philosophy of the Act*, University of Chicago Press, Chicago, 1938, p. 144.

naturalistic investigation of conscious phenomena rather than away from it, and they tend to re-enforce criticism of the classic fragmentation and bifurcation of the world into the explainable and the unexplainable. It is this that made Dewey feel that the functional concept of mind could institute a veritable revolution:

> The old center was mind knowing by means of an equipment of powers complete within itself, and merely exercised upon an antecedent external material equally complete in itself. The new center is indefinite interactions taking place within a course of nature which is not fixed and complete, but which is capable of direction to new and different results through the mediation of intentional operations. (9:290-91)

We have concentrated on what appears to be Dewey's chief contribution to psychology, and not only to psychology; but in conclusion we should list without elaboration some of his other interests. These appear principally in his early *Human Nature and Conduct* (1922), the chief point of which is to celebrate the place of habit in conduct and, in a 'behavioristic' way, to elevate environment and conditioning over impulse. Habit dominates, at least in this book, his ethics as well as his psychology; it becomes almost the unit of psychological analysis as, in ethics, it seems to stand for the very definition of character. This emphasis on habit is unquestionably consistent with Dewey's constant underscoring of the social aspect of conduct, but it becomes a little strained from time to time when he pushes the argument to what amounts to a political and not merely a social interpretation of habit and character. Also emphasized in the book is the malleability of human nature through control of habit and therefore ultimately through education; this, also, will be returned to later.

But in *Human Nature and Conduct,* as elsewhere, there are evident weaknesses in Dewey's handling of the human personality which cannot be passed over—weaknesses, incidentally, which he himself has acknowledged.* Foremost would be an underlying assumption or rather mood of healthy-mindedness—not that there is anything wrong in healthy-mindedness. But it is this, perhaps more than anything else, that tends to date Dewey. There is almost nothing in his writings of anxiety, loneliness, anguish. The distressing experiences of humans all seem socially determined and socially controllable. Now this itself is not a theoretical weakness, at least if one accepts the interpersonal approach to psychology and psychiatry; but lack of reference to personal torment and individual frustration makes for a certain thinness and unrealism in Dewey's writings. One is not expecting him to be an existentialist—although in a fellow pragmatist, William James, there is more than a little soul-searching—but one does miss, at least in these days, a necessary touch of forlornness. Putting it differently—and Dewey has himself admitted this—there is no developed theory of individual personality in his psychology.

Akin to this is Dewey's underplaying of Freud, whose ideas are referred to only casually. (Indeed, one of the infrequent references to psychoanalysis seems to be a little extreme: 'Upon this point at least a Marxian simplification is nearer the truth than that of Jung.' 6: 154.) Yet, as Mead himself recognized, a Freudian (or at least a neo-

* Cf. 19: 554–6.

Freudian) approach provides a significant complement to the social theory of the self. Again, as Allport notices, there is almost nothing in Dewey that deals with the influences of infancy upon personality—this despite his enormous contribution to education, even at the kindergarten level. Perhaps Dewey's only experimental paper in psychology, back in 1894, was on children's language, and yet what happens in the pre-linguistic period seems not to have been reckoned with.

If these are indeed limitations and gaps, they need to be recognized; but they withdraw nothing from the impressiveness of Dewey's analysis of mind. It may be that such an analysis does not have to vary from Age to Age—one of Anxiety, now of Security, next of . . . —instead it may be that the symbolic, linguistic, and in *that* sense social interpretation will prove to be the constant factor a science of human nature demands.

8. Intelligence and Liberalism

If John Dewey's philosophy seems dated, it is most evident today in the field of politics. At the moment 'liberalism' seems almost a smear word. The 'new conservatism' has taken over and the range it supposedly covers is staggering in its extent, omitting no one, not even labor leaders or erstwhile New Dealers. Yet no discussion of Dewey's social and political theories could be complete or even meaningful without an attempt to understand the liberal position he represented, perhaps more than anyone else in American public life, or without a companion attempt to examine that liberal position to see if it has a permanent appeal beyond what may be only a political vogue.

It should already be evident that Dewey's social philosophy cannot be a mere adjunct to a system, much less something tacked on to satisfy latter-day liberals. In a fundamental sense philosophy itself, both as analytical tool and as cultural product, is for Dewey social. As we have seen, he uses the category 'social' to locate the very dimension of mind, as well as to help provide the context and almost the definition of thinking, scientific method, knowledge, and value, all of which depend upon the symbolized relationships and transactions among men. And as was noted at the outset of our discussion, Dewey regards the philosophic enterprise itself as an aspect of culture, as a social phenomenon and not simply the work 'of lonely though brilliant thinkers.' This argument (found principally in the opening chapters of his *Reconstruction in Philosophy* and in his article on 'Philosophy' in the *Encyclopaedia of the Social Sciences*) holds philosophy to be the agent, as it was in ancient Greece, which brings to consciousness the problems bound to arise in any self-critical culture. Moreover, the classic problems, he feels, are ultimately value problems and these, in turn, are the problems arising from man's relations to his fellows.

But the use of 'social' as a philosophical category might appear precious were it not also to be considered in the more prosaic sense in which—for better or worse—it has usually been opposed to 'individual.' This kind of contraposition has been the burden of most of the current strictures against 'security,' 'conformity,' 'the organization man,' and 'groupiness' in general. Some critics have attributed 'the lost individual' to various socially oriented philosophies, and a few of the writers have been rash enough to include the name of Dewey. Perhaps they have been careless rather than rash, for Dewey's persistent attack on the conformist has been almost a classic, occupying two or three books and large sections of others, the general theme of which is that he wants more, not fewer, truly rugged individuals. 'There is more danger at present,' he wrote, 'that the genuinely creative effort of the individual will be lost than there is of any return to earlier individualism. Everything makes for the mass.' To which he adds, 'Men who are balked of a legitimate realization of their subjectivity . . . will compensate by finding release within their inner consciousness.' (7:240–41.) Again, 'Conformity is a name for the absence of vital interplay; the arrest and benumbing of communication . . . It is the artificial substitute used to hold men together in lack of associations that are incorporated into inner dispositions of thought and desire.'

(10:85–6.) To include Dewey among those who have been seduced by the magic of the group is as short-sighted as to see him a representative of laissez-faire individualism.

This running battle between the Individual and Society results, at least in part, from the reliance on bloodless abstractions, more incorrigible in politics than elsewhere. Dewey's point is that the persistent use of vacuous abstractions, say Individual and Society, has done a work of untold mischief in deflecting the course of social thinking. When 'individual' or 'society' is looked upon as something in itself and factitiously separate; when the two are urged to cooperate or to remain opposed; when it is graciously admitted that in reality their interests are mutual—then we are in the land of dialectic. We are using general ideas to solve particular problems. And that, for Dewey, is inexcusable.

As soon as the Individual is regarded as a general idea, he becomes something aloof, discrete, insulated, not to say amputated. But when individuals are specifically located, a different class of problem arises and questions like these become relevant: *Which* individuals will be aided or harmed by this or that act? How will they be affected? Why are they in situations that make their being harmed or aided a problem? What will happen to other individuals as a result of what happens to them? Questions of this kind may not be easy to answer; in many cases they cannot possibly be answered with our present knowledge. But unless this is the direction in which attention is turned, questions such as these will never be answered.

In a complementary fashion, Society must be particularized. Since society covers 'street gangs, schools for burglary, clans, social cliques, trades unions, joint stock corporations, villages and international alliances,' it has no meaning until, like individuals, it is localized. (5:200.) *Which* social groups should perform this or that task? In what way should a group approach its task? What other groups or individuals will be affected? Should specific groups expand or contract their jurisdiction? Again, these may be the most perplexing of questions. Yet they can be translated into inquiries with content and thus reach out to the developing sciences of man. Problems about Society never can.*

A second demurrer against the traditional opposition of individual and social is, of course, to be found in Dewey's now familiar idea of transaction. Used in the present context, it suggests that individuals, like minds, emerge from a social situation; they are indeed made and remade, although not by some monolithic force called Society. These relations are among individuals, not between Individual and Society. If they are mutually constitutive, as they are, it is simply that man is a social animal, not an animal that *becomes* social. 'Individuals who are not bound together in associations, whether domestic, economic, religious, political, artistic, or educational, are monstrosities. It is absurd to suppose that the ties which hold them together are merely external and do not react into mentality and character, producing the framework of personal disposition.' This is Dewey talking (10:81–2), but it could be any philosopher who believes that man is by nature a social animal. In any case, this cannot be taken as further evidence of what some have termed the dominance of the 'social ethic'—or of the depression of individuality. Nor need his observations

* See 8 for an extended development of this particular point of view.

about man's social nature be twisted into a form in which 'social' is made to picture something out of *1984*. Rather, they reflect the fact that man does extend beyond his skin. That individuals are separate, alone, and sometimes frightened by being alone is not the discovery of existentialist psychology. Such loneliness, whether celebrated or deplored, is itself part of a transaction.

Dewey is trying 'to get away from the influence of belief in bald single forces, whether they are thought of as intrinsically psychological or sociological' (16:39) If he proceeds to substitute for 'bald single forces' his notion of transaction, it is not because the word is magical. It does seem, however, to provide antisepsis against the infectious appeal of one-way causation (whatever the direction) and against the substitution of bodiless generalizations for the specific give-and-take that goes to make up the actual individual.

Dewey next goes on to argue that, like the individual, the idea of individualism has also arrived at the particular position it occupies at a particular time because of certain historical developments. The usual interpretation of individualism as exclusively a negative and laissez-faire philosophy emerged from the background of the seventeenth and eighteenth centuries, and it revealed a consistent pattern of political, economic, and religious forces. Here were new economic classes achieving new political power, a new religion for a new class, new nations coming into existence while others were changing their entire orientation, new technological energies of a superrevolutionary character. The impact was largely protestant, in all fields not simply the religious, and there was nothing unctuous—as there tends to be in present-day political revivalism—about the laissez-faire individualism which emerged. There were good reasons for suspicion of a strong state dominated by anachronistic legal power, suspicion directed as well against states of affairs going beyond the political. Nor was there anything merely parochial or transient about the philosophy of natural rights and hands off the individual: to reaffirm the perennial appeal of political democracy, personal freedom, and, above all, civil liberties—when it is not cant—is to outline the very assumptions of the modern age. Indeed, the assumptions are claimed as basic by both the latter-day liberals and the new conservatives.

But having carefully acknowledged all this, a thinker like Dewey must go on to argue that a general shift in emphasis from negative to positive needs to be engineered if individualism is ever to outgrow the inevitable limitations and restrictions of a particular historical environment. By 'negative' he has in mind the classic formula: let men alone, free them from legal inequalities, allow them to grow naturally, and they will develop as a rational Nature meant them to. In such a context, 'positive' is understood as implying that it is not enough to let men alone. The values of a genuine individualism cannot be automatically achieved; they do not rise up with the mere removal of restraint. The individual cannot achieve educational equality by being left alone, he cannot win economic security by being left alone, he cannot participate in the political, industrial, and cultural life of his society by being left alone. 'Being left alone' is an idea that has had a narcotic effect upon too many self-styled and, for Dewey, old-styled individualists. If, as Dewey says, 'the only creative individuality is that of mind,' certainly this above all puts in a claim for the opportunity to be nurtured and to develop, an opportunity not ordinarily found just lying around. It needs to be provided.

This shift from negative to positive is the theme of *Individualism—Old and New* (1930) and also of *Liberalism and Social Action.* (1935) But the theme will be seriously misinterpreted if it is understood as an all-out abandonment of laissez-faire. One of Dewey's three ingredients of liberalism is, of course, liberty itself; and in at least one area of individual experience—that of the civil liberties—the laissez-faire argument still exercises (or should exercise) the power it held for the eighteenth century. Injunctions against the state, hands off the individual, no government interference —these slogans are still dynamite when they are used to defend a Bill of Rights. Yet even here, in the concept of rights itself, there has also been a notable shift. We need only mention the evolution of the concept from the classical notion of rights as inherent and metaphysical elements of a naturally asocial individual to the more modern interpretation of rights as claims made by an individual upon society.* These are claims for the opportunities without which an individual cannot develop his legitimate potentialities (a development that Dewey lists as a second ingredient of liberalism). Rights evolve from metaphysical entities to moral demands, in the course of which they also change, at least in part, from negative to positive. Compare the traditional rights of the seventeenth and eighteenth centuries with those found in the United Nations Charter and the various 'new' bills of rights prominent in this

* A summary of this kind of development may be found in George R. Geiger's *Philosophy and the Social Order*, Boston, Houghton Mifflin, 1947; pp. 277–89.

country at least since the New Deal and in Europe since World War II. To be sure, there are still the 'negative' rights—the freedoms 'from'—but there are also the freedoms 'for.' Freedom *from* ignorance, disease, and insecurity is at the same time a claim *for* knowledge, health, and the various forms of stability; and this kind of claim is idle without the aid and interposition of specific social agencies. This was not necessarily the case when the doctrine of natural rights was formulated; indeed, it was a tragedy for political liberalism that the negative character of rights was frozen, as it were, on the very eve of the Industrial Revolution and so has yielded only with the greatest difficulty to the economic and technological changes which have made so much of laissez-faire simply an anachronism. In any event, it is this shift from a passive reliance on the bare efforts of natural men to the more prosperous cooperation among men—even if the form of that cooperation bears the label of 'government' or 'society'—that, for Dewey, is the occasion for what he calls the new individualism and the new liberalism.

And so we have come to the problem of liberalism. In *Liberalism and Social Action,* the third of his basic elements of liberalism is identified by Dewey as acceptance of 'the central role of free intelligence in inquiry, discussion, and expression.' It involves the substitution of scientific methods for authority in social affairs, the interest in specific means as well as in honorific ends, the general amenability of values to rational determination—and thus the connection between Dewey's general philosophy and his liberalism becomes evident. In fact, liberalism may be regarded as the application of instrumentalism to social and political problems. In an essay on Justice Holmes, which opens with Holmes's celebrated 'free trade in ideas' statement, Dewey observes that 'it [the statement] contains in spite of its brevity, three outstanding ideas: belief in the conclusions of intelligence as the finally directive force in life; in freedom of thought and expression as a condition needed in order to realize this power of direction by thought; and in the experimental character of life and thought.' He goes on to say that

> . . . as a social philosophy, 'liberalism' runs the gamut of which a vague temper of mind—often called forward-looking—is one extreme, and a definite creed as to the purposes and methods of social action is the other. The first is too vague to afford any steady guide in action; the other is so specific and fixed as to result in dogma, and thus to end in an illiberal mind. Liberalism as a method of experimentation based on insight into both social desires and actual conditions, escapes this dilemma. It signifies the adoption of the scientific habit of mind in application to social affairs.*

Now, the alleged irrelevance of such an attempted application—as irrelevant as the cognate efforts to apply intelligent inquiry to values—is what has helped to give liberalism its currently depressed position. The critics of liberalism manifest a shrewd instinct when they concentrate on its 'intellectualism' and its 'secularism' rather than upon its supposed political deficiencies: what finally turns up as the principal weakness of the liberal is his religious dereliction. This is very clear in the structures of the most pontifical of the new conservatives, Russell Kirk, but it is found as well in some of the more 'liberal' conservatives like Peter Viereck

* *Characters and Events*, edited by J. Ratner, Henry Holt, New York, 1929, Vol. I, pp. 100–101.

and Clinton Rossiter. And, of course, the apocalyptic source of the idea is Reinhold Niebuhr.

The specific indictment here is that the liberal is a naïve optimist. He has supposedly accepted the eighteenth-century belief in inevitable progress and the companion notion that man is somehow rational, good, and trustworthy; and so his philosophy—as has been said of Dewey's—is something dignified, solid, and nice, without the pity or terror of tragedy, and above all without that fear of pride which certifies the pious man. In short, the liberal neither understands nor accepts sin. Or, in more secular language, he fails to accept (it is alleged) that man is no better than he should be. Thus, when things don't work out—largely because man has been grossly overrated as a rational and intelligible animal—the liberal becomes hurt, bewildered, and, more than anything else, tired. Even when he is not tired, the liberal is said to be congenitally inactive. This is traceable to his purported habits of tentativeness, of seeing both sides of the question, of weighing issues too long and too carefully. He never makes up his mind to do anything and constantly vacillates between 'yes' and 'no,' winding up usually with an anemic 'maybe.' There is a pathetic reasonableness to his conduct which makes him pathologically wistful or, in times of crisis, dangerously obstructionist. An accompanying characteristic is his relativism. The liberal doesn't seem to believe in absolutes; therefore he can't take anything too seriously. This is the cause of his abulia, his inability to make up his mind. Was it not Earl Browder—not yet a new conservative—who defined a liberal as 'one who raises doubt and indecision to a principle'?

Such indecision results from the fact that the liberal really has no basic convictions but only working hypotheses to go by, and the resulting fecklessness can never capture the imagination or the emotions. Commitment, so the critic proposes, demands something more exciting and certain than the secular and the scientific.

It is not simply for the sake of economy or to avoid extending unduly the interminable liberal-conservative debate that we have concentrated on a single constellation of liberal inadequacies. It is rather that the suasion of the critic is nowhere more seductive and insinuating than here. More forthrightly, it is here, in the tentative and fumbling effort of human intelligence to understand itself and its limits, that the symbols of liberalism—to use a phrase of Charles Frankel's—reveal an inescapable thinness. And at certain critical periods the thinness is almost emaciation. Perhaps that was the case in the fateful spring and summer of 1939 when the present writer took the opportunity to ask John Dewey (then an advocate of American neutralism) his reactions to this type of criticism of the liberal position. The following are excerpts from Dewey's response. They are in a minor key and may not prove inspiring, but the alternatives Dewey presents need to be thoroughly examined by any non-liberal.

To my mind they [the questions] come to this: Is the disproportion between the application of the scientific experimental method to the physical conditions of human associations and its lack of application in direct social affairs such that, in the present state of the world, it is hopeless to expect a change? I know of no sweeping answer to this question. But the problem is one of degree, not of all or none. It cannot be denied that in our social life a great imbalance has resulted because the method of intelligent action has been used in determining the physical conditions that are causes of social effects, whereas it has hardly been tried in determination of social ends and values . . . In any case, the question is not, as critics have sometimes put it, one of intelligence, or knowledge, versus action, but one of *intelligent* action versus some other kind of action—whether it relies on arbitrament by violence, or 'dialectical materialistic inevitability,' on dogmas of race, blood, nationality, or supernatural guidance . . . The question is one of choice—choice between a procedure which is rigid because based on fixed dogma, and one which is flexible because based upon examination of problems actually experienced and because proposing policies as hypotheses to be experimentally tested and modified. (19:361–8, questions; 591–4, answers)

The alternatives of rigidity and flexibility presented here by Dewey point back to the concluding pages of an earlier chapter (V) on scientific method, where it was suggested that the substitution of hypothesis for the fixed idea (which in the present context, may be regarded as the ability to see both sides of the question) could well prove to be the unique contribution science will make—or could make—to civilization itself. It is not a matter at all of sweet reasonableness which dictates the tentative approach. It is simply that no other way has yet been discovered to understand and control the dramatic changes that have all but overwhelmed man in the few centuries following first the scientific and then the technological revolutions. It has been argued that except for the invention of fire nothing has happened to man of more significance than these revolutions. Nothing has brought about more constant and profound alteration in every aspect of his life. To handle these revolutionary changes—not to mention the whole concept of evolution itself—science has had to develop the flexibility so conspicuously absent from pre-scientific inquiry and still conspicuously absent from those regions of experience held to be outside the precincts of science. It is simply that a rigid and doctrinaire method would be unable to grasp the world, either the natural world of gradual change or the technological world of revolution. 'The pure conservative,' said Whitehead, 'is fighting against the very essence of the universe,' whereas scientific liberalism institutionalizes revolution (as George Mead said of democracy itself). The hypothetical approach is a strategy of understanding and control, not primarily a principle of morals. This is indeed a premise of John Stuart Mill in his still relevant essay on *Liberty* (which, incidentally, like *On the Origin of Species*, appeared during the year of Dewey's birth).

Let us put the same thing another way. Criticism of the liberal attitude of hypothesis and tentativeness seems itself to rest on an assumption that unless there is absolute certainty nothing can be done. Without certainty there can be only (liberal) fumbling, hesitation, and general impotence. Now, it is not enough to say that such an assumption is the philosophical basis of any form of totalitarianism. More to the point, such an assumption is simply unfounded. The constipated notion that tentativeness of judgment means suspension of action has been repudiated by a methodology which has made more things move than has any other force in Western culture. But when action is initiated on a less-than-certainty basis, provision is made for the 'minority' hypothesis. Even though, as one of a number of multiple working suggestions, it is not at the moment being acted upon, an idea is not liquidated but is ready to serve as a future substitute for a rejected or unsuccessful theory. There is a tolerance here that often is missing elsewhere.

What Bertrand Russell has said of the function of philosophy might be applied to the contribution of science and of liberalism, that it 'can teach us to live without certainty yet without being paralyzed by hesitation.'

Of another characteristic indictment of the liberal, his naïve optimism, let it be said clearly (as Dewey has said many times) that there is here no eighteenth-century belief in necessary progress, much less a dialectical conviction of inevitable triumph. Nature is what it is; it is neither good nor bad in general. It is a fit subject for neither moral praise nor blame but, in a Baconian sense, for 'exploitation'—which, as has been made abundantly clear, in no way precludes an appreciative, esthetic, or even a pious reaction to the natural scene. Nature need not be approached optimistically or pessimistically; what William James called 'meliorism' would be a more appropriate response of the liberal. The natural world and the social world present a challenge; they can be changed and they have been. The working assumption of liberalism—as it is of science—is simply that the world presents the possibilities for direction. There is no unbridled optimism in this any more than in the liberal's ostensible faith in human reason. This, in turn, is simply the recognition that man *does* solve problems through reflective thinking, that scientific inquiry is an instrument which the human animal has developed. It has not solved all problems and never will; there is here no blind reliance on the omnicompetence of a simple and absolute reason, such as may have hypnotized the eighteenth century. Disillusion with the rationalism of an Age of Reason cannot legitimately apply to the more modest position which simply sees no generally acceptable alternative to free intelligence as the solver of human problems, an intelligence, moreover, which fits into the pattern of an entire human personality and is not exclusively 'intellectualistic' in some now suspect sense.

We need now to turn to the economic and political dimensions of liberalism, although it must constantly be kept in mind that liberalism is not solely a matter of economic or political dimension; it is concerned with the general enrichment of the individual and may relate to his education, his religion, his thinking, his esthetic creativeness and appreciation. The economic phase of Dewey's new liberalism revolves around the theme that intelligence and scientific inquiry, as applied to social problems, demand the use of planning, a word he introduced as early as 1918.* Indeed the change from an unplanned to a planned economy is what he has termed the crisis of liberalism. Now, the word 'planning,' it needs to be recognized, has tended to produce a kind of semantic block. On the one hand, it provokes the stereotyped reactions which associate planning with socialism, communism, bureaucracy, and contrast it with free enterprise, the American way, individualism, and even piety. On the other hand, the word seems to some to have a magic and to be able by itself—such is the magic of great words and phrases—to solve our problems. Of course, all of us are constantly 'planning' something—a party, a trip, a marriage, a life, or a life insurance. But when the planning becomes public there is noticeable resistance. The kind of intelligent foresight which is accepted in every aspect of life

* In an article 'Elements of Social Reorganization,' reprinted in *Characters and Events: Popular Essays in Social and Political Philosophy*, edited by J. Ratner, Henry Holt, New York, 1929, Vol. II, pp. 745–59.

becomes then either malicious and dangerous, or the sign of a special and superior emancipation. This ambivalence about a short, familiar word is unhelpful. One of the things Dewey was trying to get across in his books of the depression period and earlier was the idea that concepts—whether 'planning' or 'free enterprise'—never by themselves solve anything. Only the reading of a book like *Characters and Events* which is composed largely of articles written by Dewey for the *New Republic* during his long connection with that periodical, can show how he attempted, in what otherwise might be considered the most trivial of cases, to apply specific and even parochial plans to the issues of the time. This was no mere celebration of planning; and even though some of his contributions now seem not only dated but occasionally misguided, the suggested hypotheses and experiments are a clear indication of what amounted to a new approach to politics.

At the same time Dewey was also trying to suggest a series of principles about planning something like the following (although these are not his words): that it is possible for human intelligence to intervene decisively in the course of human affairs; that planning is a way of solving problems, not a completely predetermined program; that planning is indeed forced upon man by changing economic and technological conditions; but that the direction of the planning is still his option.

This last point is no more than a recognition of the fact that a post-industrial culture is necessarily a planned one, the option being whether the planning be public or private. Yet this fact, which can hardly be denied, is obscured by what Lewis Mumford has called a 'pseudomorph,' a cultural hangover or lag: man's institutions and mores have lapsed far behind the pace set by technology, and the social passwords which once gave him entrance to the pre-industrial mysteries have lost their magic without being discarded; they have become folklore. According to Dewey, old-fashioned liberalism closed its eyes to these changes and kept wishing for the bygone days, whereas the new liberal must adjust to what in some form or other is already a collectivist society.

Why then, if labels are indeed important, is Dewey regarded as a liberal rather than as a socialist? This, of course, introduces a large problem which can only be touched upon here. For one thing, if 'socialism' can be distinguished from 'Marxism'—as it must be, although the terminological difficulties are now almost insuperable—then Dewey certainly can be regarded as a democratic socialist, say, of the British Labour Party variety (at least of that very large non-Marxist section of the party and the affiliated trades unions) or of that of the more pronounced New Deal theoreticians.* But, except for a period in the 1930s when at least one aspect of Marxism, economic determinism, played a conspicuous part in his writings, Dewey cannot be said to have been a Marxist; and of course his later attacks on Marx were decisive. Moreover, except for a few years immediately

* In a letter to Jim Cork, which unfortunately is not given a date, Dewey wrote: 'I think that on the basis of *Liberalism and Social Action,* and to some extent *Individualism—Old and New,* I can be classed as a democratic socialist. If I were permitted to define "socialism" and "socialist" I would so classify myself today . . .' This is found (p. 349) in an article by Cork, 'Dewey and Karl Marx,' in the volume, *John Dewey: Philosopher of Science and Freedom,* edited by Sidney Hook, Dial, New York, 1950. This chapter, along with some of the early work of Hook, is perhaps the chief effort to ally Dewey not merely with socialism, but with the Marxist philosophy itself.

following the Russian Revolution, when Dewey visited the Soviet Union, helped with their revised school system, and became for a while the leading American intellectual championing the recognition of Russia, he has always been disenchanted with the rigid, anti-democratic religion which passes there and elsewhere for socialism. Because of this long-time disenchantment Dewey could not go along with many other liberals during their unhappy and tragic popular-front period.

In relating Dewey to Marx, we need first to separate Marxism from Soviet communism. (Some Marxists, like Jim Cork, believe that Dewey was himself unable to make that separation.) Even if one confines himself to the canon of Marx-Engels writings, and to some of the classical exegesis, it would still be impossible to come out with a kind of litmus paper the pinkness of which would determine an orthodox Marxist. For at the very least Marxism is a complex of ideas, some of which have at times been emphasized more than others. There is, for instance, a philosophy of history, economic determinism; next, an item of classical political economy, the labor theory of value, to which is added the exciting amendment of surplus value and the exploitation of labor; then, a political interpretation of the state as an organ of class oppression culminating in a doctrine of revolution; over all, there is a metaphysic, dialectical materialism, with its concept of the clash between opposites and its secular application in the class struggle. This list is by no means exhaustive, yet it may indicate that although Marxism is indeed a complex in which constituent parts do intermesh, some of the items are unquestionably independent variables.

Take the economic determination of history. Acceptance

of such an interpretation is a necessary but certainly not a sufficient reason to make one a Marxist. Both Plato and Aristotle embraced the theory in part, not to mention Alexander Hamilton and James Madison (*Federalist* No. 10 is perhaps the most succinct and cogent statement of economic determinism to be found anywhere) as well as the classical economists, to whom one might go on to add Henry George, Charles Beard, and a host of others, including Dewey. Mentioning only a few of his books, and not considering the great number of articles dealing with the theme, we find the opening chapter of *Reconstruction in Philosophy* (1920) giving not only an economic but even a class interpretation of the origins of philosophic dualism in ancient Greece; in *Human Nature and Conduct* (1922) there is at times an almost bald development of psychology in strictly economic terms; and, as we have already seen, in *Liberalism and Social Action* (1935) and *Individualism—Old and New* (1930) the economic factor is the key to a new politics. Indeed, there is one sentence in the *Liberalism* book (page 48) which may have given Dewey pause later: '. . . the formal concept of liberty loses its meaning under a classless society.' The point here is simply that one aspect of the Marxist complex is to a degree accepted—although never as a single causative factor—by Dewey; but this of course establishes nothing more than the fact that both Marx and Dewey at times accepted by and large an economic interpretation of history.*

* In the chapter by Jim Cork, mentioned on a previous page, there is an extended attempt—pages 338–41—to itemize the specific points of agreement between Marx and Dewey, but this kind of listing suffers in general from the undistributed middle. That Marx and Dewey, for example, both believed in a world in process means no more than that both Marx and Dewey believed in a world in process. So did Heraclitus, Darwin, Hegel,

If there is anything decisive in determining a Marxist—and this is simply a suggestion—it would seem to be acceptance of the encouragement of inevitable class struggle as the determining force in social change. It is this doctrine which appears to tie together in a meaningful and programmatic way the metaphysical, historical, economic, and political aspects of the philosophy. And it is precisely this doctrine which is repudiated by the liberal, and not only by the liberal. Hamilton and Madison, second to none in their recognition of factional strife, regarded the state as a mitigator of such struggle and not as an abettor. And Dewey, even in his most provocative work during the depression years, always took particular care to attack the idea of inevitable and omniscient class struggle and to reject totally this aspect of Marxism. Liberalism is above all, he writes, the mediation of social transition. This is not some tepid, middle-of-the-road policy any more than is mediation in any situation; it is rather a recognition of the general technique by which problems become amenable to intelligent decision.* The alternatives to intelligent mediation, Dewey proceeds to point out, are fanatical dogmatism on the one hand or drift and casual improvisation on the other.

Dewey's principal criticism of Marxism is found in the fourth chapter of *Freedom and Culture* (1939). It centers, as might be expected, on his refusal to accept metaphysical explanation for social and political problems. The dialectic,

---

Bergson, and Whitehead, to go no further. From this type of general agreement no legitimate argument can be extended to something more specific.

* In his suggestion of 'creative bargaining,' Max Otto has developed in a most important way this point of Dewey's. So did the late Horace S. Fries, in work which unfortunately was never completed.

the class struggle, the labor theory—these are as abstract as any of the Hegelianisms or economic classicisms from which they derive. There is no cosmic reason why capitalism *must* give rise to communism via socialism, why collectivism *must* be achieved by means of a revolutionary technique, why surplus value *must* arise, why *any* abstract sequence *must* appear. Marxism is primarily 'a logic of general notions.' It is an illustration of what Karl Popper calls 'historicism,' the monolithic reliance on a solitary factor of explanation, solitary and inexpugnable. 'The practical techniques derived from the Marxist single all-embracing law of a single causative force follow the pattern discarded in scientific inquiry and in scientific engineering.' (16:86.) Such an all-embracing law must also be discarded by any kind of democratic social philosophy, and Dewey criticizes Marx for being insensitive (except in a few kind references to the Anglo-American political system) to the significance of democracy and, conversely, to the totalitarian potential in socialism itself, which developed so tragically in Italian fascism, German Naziism, and Russian Communism.

In other writings, Dewey used some of the now familiar criticisms of Marxism, such as its historical and scientific inaccuracies, a few of them spectacular; the general 'old-fashionedness' of Marx's economic theory, confining itself, as it necessarily did, to the paleotechnic phase of the Industrial Revolution; and, above all, the possibility of the middle class itself—expanding so rapidly in this neotechnic generation although it was doomed to extinction by Marxist orthodoxy—becoming the vehicle of a 'socialism' quite different from the classical variety and thus affording one of the exciting non-Marxist possibilities of the second half of the twentieth century. Finally, as to Soviet Communism (which, to repeat, must always be separated from the generic meanings of socialism and even of Marxism) Dewey's complete disillusion came with the Trotzky trials which, in the interests of justice and honesty, forced the philosopher to his celebrated Mexican investigations.*

To say that Dewey is 'the philosopher of democracy' can become a cliché, as can the word 'democracy' itself. At the same time it would be too much to expect here a fresh statement, giving to democracy, as it were, a local and vicarious

* The clearest and most economical account of this Mexican affair will be found in the paper by the novelist James T. Farrell, which appears as the last chapter in the Hook symposium (op. cit.). It was Dewey's efforts in helping to show that the trials were the first of the many Soviet frame-ups that made him the public enemy number 1 of Russian philosophy. For, it must be remembered, this could be regarded as particularly unfriendly, since Dewey had been an early friend of the Soviet Union and also had seemed to be writing from a Marxist point of view. In any case, notice the following item from the *Large Soviet Encyclopaedia*, 1952, 2nd ed., Vol. XV, pp. 343–4: 'John Dewey—a reactionary bourgeois philosopher and sociologist, a subjective idealist . . . While ideologically serving the interests of aggressive American imperialism, Dewey worked out a variation of pragmatism called instrumentalism . . . Any view or fanciful notion which profits and pleases American imperialists can be proclaimed "scientific" and "true" with the help of this "philosophy." . . . For the bourgeoisie and their governmental workers, according to Dewey, any means are good which fortify the position of capitalism and prevent social revolution. In education, Dewey is a supporter of those methods of instruction which contribute to the rearing of energetic and enterprising defenders of capitalism who are permeated with a spirit of worship of capital and hatred toward communism. The philosophy of Dewey is a philosophy of war and fascism. Dewey is the mouthpiece of modern imperialistic reaction, the ideologist of American imperialism, a violent enemy of the *USSR*, the countries of the People's Democracy, and the revolutionary theory of Marxism-Leninism.' It is superfluous to add that this judgment has been parroted by Communist 'philosophers' everywhere, including those of the United States.

notoriety. An inventory of attitudes and practices, such as we have been outlining, is about all that can be looked for; an inventory, however, which has behind it a rich store of deeply rooted folkways. This is why, despite the philosophers and the statesmen, the idea of democracy is not easily exported or even taught.

Yet there is a basic contribution Dewey has made to the tired discussion of the meaning of democracy, and that is to connect it directly with the meaning of communication itself and, further than that, with the actual social and moral nature of man. 'Shared experience is the greatest of human goods.' This well-known sentence can be caricatured so that it seems to imply the underplaying of the individual and the glorification of the group. But what it does intend may be made clear in its context: 'Communication is consummatory as well as instrumental . . . It is instrumental as liberating us from the otherwise overwhelming pressure of events and enabling us to live in a world of things that have meaning. It is final as a sharing in the objects and arts precious to a community, a sharing whereby meanings are enhanced, deepened and solidified in the sense of communion.' (7:202, 204–5.) These shared consummations are found in the creativity of love, friendship, and art; and they, in turn, are not possible without communication among men. But such communication is based on a faith in men and their experience, a faith in the potentialities of all men. It may almost be said that democracy is not even one of the political options, since it is implicit in the very meaning of association and free communication. The Great Society must here become the Great Community.*

* This point is particularly emphasized in Dewey's *The Public and Its Problems,* especially Chapter V.

If this appears a detached or precious certification of a democratic ethic, it loses any such aura when Dewey applies his faith in the human potential to particular occasions. No liberal movement of significance and weight ever failed to enlist his ungrudging support, and no cause, however unorthodox, which proffered specific contributions and criticisms went unrecognized by him.* A bare listing of the causes to which he gave his name would fill many pages, but it might have only historical interest since much of his social pioneering—like that of so many radicals of the past—is now taken for granted. Dewey's contributions here have become commonplaces, and one doesn't get very excited about commonplaces.

Yet it may at least be mentioned that the impact of his social philosophy has been felt from the labor union to the Supreme Court. Whether it be Justice Holmes's 'pragmatic and Deweyan' approach to constitutional law (or even the case system in legal education);† or the entire development of institutional economics under men like John R. Commons; or, on the other hand, Dewey's attested work with labor leaders like Walter Reuther, David Dubinsky, and Sidney Hillman looking toward recognition of the labor union during the early days of the New Deal; or his persistent efforts to establish a new political party (one result of which may still be found in the New York City Liberal Party); or his sympathetic interest in the small earnest

* Reference should again be made to the book *Characters and Events*, which gives evidence of these multifarious interests.

† A good discussion of this point, and of the general influence of Dewey's work on the law, will be found in the chapter by Edwin L. Patterson in the Hook symposium, op. cit.

movements on the fringe of liberal action—nothing which seemed to show signs of democratic promise fell outside his attention. If his concern with liberal causes seemed omnivorous—occasionally finding itself therefore with a case of indigestion—this was a risk foreseen by his experimental attitude. There had to be specification and follow-through if his social philosophy was relevant; yet no guarantee of success could be posted—except that of continuing education. For there could be no divorce of democracy from education.

At the opening of the present chapter it was suggested that liberalism is for the moment out of fashion. Yet fashions change. Although Irwin Edman did not regard himself as a prophet, he said in his calm way of Dewey that, in social philosophy, 'his was a voice of reasonableness and imagination and it will be heard again.'

9. Some Outcomes for Education

It has been said that John Dewey could not be elected today to any school board in the country. Even if something of an exaggeration, the statement is indicative of a wide-spread reaction against 'progressive' education—or what has passed for it. Dewey himself shared in that reaction, at least against what came to pass for progressive education. But what is it that he and others are reacting to? What is the 'newer' education, whatever else it may be called? In *Experience and Education*, published in 1938, Dewey stated that although he was by no means repudiating the label of 'progressive' he did prefer a more neutral term like 'newer.' 'Progressive,' like 'pragmatism,' had become freighted with too many misconceptions. There are a number of ways to describe this newer education. One of them, suggested by Dewey himself, would consist of a series of alternative positions in which the 'old' education is contrasted with the new. However, in doing this he takes great pains to deprecate such alternatives if they are to be understood as a series of clean disjunctions; in fact, the following passage is in the context of rejecting an either-or approach that would set off irretrievably and without exception one kind of education against another kind:

> To imposition from above is opposed expression and cultivation of individuality; to learning from texts and teachers, learning through experience; to acquisition of isolated skills and techniques by drill is opposed acquisition of them as means of attaining ends which make direct vital appeal; to preparation for a more or less remote future is opposed making the most of the

opportunities of present life; to static aims and materials is opposed acquaintance with a changing world. (15: 5–6.)

In his early *Democracy and Education,* Dewey proposed another set of criteria:

We may say that the kind of experience to which the work of the schools should contribute is one marked by executive competency in the management of resources and obstacles encountered (efficiency); by sociability, or interest in the direct companionship of others; by aesthetic taste or capacity to appreciate artistic excellence in at least some of its classic forms; by trained intellectual method, or interest in some mode of scientific achievement; and by sensitiveness to the rights and claims of others—conscientiousness. (3: 285–6.)

Other items could be added to complete the description. They would include the role the school has come to play as itself a social institution, as a community not cut off from but inherently part of an ongoing cultural process, contributing directly to that process and, in turn, basing its curriculum significantly upon it. Then, there are other characteristic features, such as the emphasis upon student initiative—at all ages of education; the constant stress upon the art of teaching; the general persuasion that, to quote John Brubacher, the individual being educated must learn 'to choose more responsibly what he wants to do in a social setting with the fullest regard for the consequences.' Above all, there is the focusing on the individual child, with the educator as physician and counselor as well as teacher; the conviction that a democratic education devoted to the cultivation of individuality and to the true enrichment of the experience of every man will cherish the child as an authentic person and not as only a step to something else.

It is clear that ideas like these are not to be credited, or debited, uniquely to John Dewey. They fit into a revolution in education going back at least to Rousseau, and many of them were already operating in this country when Dewey founded his Laboratory School at the University of Chicago in 1896; other similar ideas were later put into practice quite independently of him. Nevertheless, the stereotype of Dewey as the father of progressive education seems to be a permanent one and in many circles, both here and abroad, he is therefore classed not as 'philosopher' but as 'educator' or 'educationist'—and so can be dismissed quite cavalierly.

It seems equally clear that although all the above items would not be generally accepted, they do seem eminently plausible. That is to say, few educators today would care to assert all the first alternatives given in the opening quotation, or to contravert all the criteria of the second, or to regard the child as something to be exploited. The controversy seems rather to be located—at least for the opponents of the newer education—in the means whereby these admittedly honorable (if sometimes challenged) ends are to be achieved. For the neutral in education (should there be any) or for one more or less sympathetic to the Dewey position, the problem is located differently. It is linked to the excesses and misinterpretations which have conspired to give allegedly progressive education the reputation it has in some quarters, debiting it for nothing less than juvenile delinquency, illiteracy, anti-intellectualism, and even 'barbarism.' Distortions of the newer education have been the constant concern of Dewey and of others. In *Experience and Education,* which was one of Dewey's major efforts to rescue his philosophy of education from some of the more bizarre interpretations of it, the following passage follows close after the one already quoted:

> A philosophy which proceeds on the basis of rejection, of sheer opposition, will . . . tend to suppose that because the old education was based on readymade organization, therefore it suffices to reject organization *in toto,* instead of striving to discover what it means and how it is to be attained on the basis of experience . . . When external authority is rejected, it does not follow that all authority should be rejected, but rather that there is need to search for a more effective source of authority. (15: 7–8.)

Dewey is here putting his finger on one of the fertile sources of educational distortion, the anarchy resulting from sheer rejection. There are other sources. One is found in a sentimental cult of the child stemming from some of the Rousseauan exaggerations: because of this, undue concentration on the needs of the child has often led in the school to an abdication of teacher responsibility and to a resulting spirit of anti-intellectualism. Another source is the confusion of improvisation with experiment. Still another is the absence of a consistent social philosophy to provide a rationale and justification for educational practices that, without such a philosophy, are 'democratic' only in a loose and uncritical sense.* In general, the sources of the extravagancies that have helped to give the newer education its bad press are to be found in the failure of the educator to ground his program on a secure theoretical base; the absence of such a base has resulted in a disconnected series of educational

* This point has been made particularly by Boyd Bode, one of the outstanding early theorists of the new education, in his *Progressive Education at the Crossroads,* Newson, Chicago and New York, 1938.

'experiments' which sometimes have turned out to be only gadgets, occasionally with a boomerang effect.

This possible absence of a developed philosophy of education has had unfortunate results. One of them has been the patronizing and derisive dismissal of 'education' on the part of many professional philosophers and teachers of the liberal arts and the sciences; indeed such a peremptory act of dismissal virtually certifies the dismisser as a scholar and gentleman. Of more concern is the fact, in Dewey's words, that many modern philosophers do not take 'education with sufficient seriousness for it to occur to them that any rational person could actually think it possible that philosophizing should focus about education as the supreme human interest in which, moreover, other problems, cosmological, moral, logical, come to a head.'*

In other words, more than a philosophy *of* education is involved. Indeed, education may even help to locate and to define the general enterprise of philosophy, as is suggested in this well-known statement by Dewey:

> If we are willing to conceive education as the process of forming fundamental dispositions, intellectual and emotional, toward nature and fellowmen, philosophy may even be defined as *the general theory of education.* Unless a philosophy is to remain symbolic—or verbal—or a sentimental indulgence for the few, or else mere arbitrary dogma, its auditing of past experience and its program of values must take effect in conduct . . . In fact, education offers a vantage ground from which to penetrate to the human, as distinct from the technical, significance of philosophic discussion. (3:383; italics in original.)

* In *Contemporary American Philosophy,* edited by G. P. Adams and W. P. Montague, Macmillan, New York, 1930, Vol. II, p. 23.

It is this intimate connection between philosophy and education which must be kept in mind in any discussion of Dewey and the newer education, for his views on education are inseparable from his general philosophy. In one sense they may be viewed as corollaries of his major principles, even if, in time, much of his educational thinking preceded the establishment of his overall philosophic position. In another sense, as in the above quotation, the emphasis seems almost to be reversed. But in either case no special place has to be found for philosophy or education, and no artificial constraint is needed to keep them together. This becomes particularly clear when Dewey proposes his 'technical definition of education: It is that reconstruction or organization of experience which adds to the meaning of experience, and which increases ability to direct the course of subsequent experience.' (3:89–90) Of course the key word here is, again, 'experience.' Although the meaning of the term for Dewey (and its appropriateness) have already been discussed, a brief summary here may help to provide a perspective from which to look at the newer education.

The following elements need to be kept in mind, if only as a bare inventory: (1) The word 'experience' stands for a special kind of existence, related to existence or nature as part is to whole. (2) Although experience certainly involves and is related to the operation of a nervous system and the appearance of consciousness, this does not imply two discrete realms of 'objective' and 'subjective.' Experience is always to be understood as a process rather than as a thing, as an organic transaction rather than as the contents of a container. (3) Within experience there may be indeterminacies and therefore problems—which are the very source of thinking and of consciousness itself—but experience as such cannot meaningfully be denigrated, just as, on the other hand, it cannot be allowed to swallow the world in one idealistic gulp. Since experience extends from the trivial, casual, and blind to the incandescence which illuminates everything men prize, it entails discrimination, choice, meaning, and quality; it is not to be wallowed in sentimentally any more than it is to be chastened as somehow unreal. Selectivity always must play a part in helping to achieve that richness, completeness, and consummation of experience which serves for Dewey as the only authentic moral direction.

It is this last point which clearly connects experience to education, for just any old experience is not necessarily educative or even valuable. Indeed, 'any experience is miseducative that has the effect of arresting or distorting the the growth of further experience.' (15:13) This line not only challenges what, in some quarters, has been mistaken for progressive education, but it also may serve to introduce those elements of educational experience that lead to growth and completeness.

If educational experience, like all experience, is indeed a process and a transaction, then it is in some sense active, and the experiencing organism is not a passive receiver but a dynamic participant in a moving, developing situation. But there is nothing in such an observation to indicate activity or movement simply for the sake of activity and movement, and certainly nothing to indicate one-sided activity such, say, as that of the child alone. Yet this kind of interpretation has become an educational cliché. The child is an integral part of the transaction, but so is the teacher, the school, and the general social situation stretching beyond the school. Mere activity, undirected and unilateral, is of no more educational importance, Dewey insists, than is a sneeze or any other free impulsive 'expression.' But when impulses are blocked and a resulting problem develops, then directed, purposeful, and intelligent activity is demanded to overcome the problem, activity which now carries the weightiest of educational burdens.

Without developing the detailed educational implementation of purposive activity which Dewey calls for and gives in his many educational writings, we may nevertheless establish that a philosophy of experience has significant educational implications, but not necessarily the ones which always have been drawn. Specifically, the implication that an enriched experience must actively involve the organism (the child, in this particular case) and not allow it to become a passive receptacle is one that is easily and correctly drawn. What also must follow, however, is that this activity and freedom is not just random movement. If activity and freedom are to have educational import, they need to illustrate a developing self-control, power to judge and evaluate, ability to use ideas—in a word, the *intelligent* activity of problem solving.

Just as routine and mechanical activity is non-educative or miseducative, so is meaningless activity, activity which does not lead to something beyond itself. It is certain to become narrow and more than likely to lead to an underplaying of intelligent activity. Such an underplaying has become a stock criticism of progressive education, but it can in no way apply to Dewey's position. In an earlier chapter, we already have had occasion to discuss his handling of logic and reflective thinking. It needs to be pointed out here that his little *How We Think,* which first appeared in 1910, has as its subtitle 'A Restatement of the Relation of Reflective Thinking to the Educative Process,' and that one of its aims was to encourage rational activity in the school. Now, one of the main planks in a platform of what today passes for anti-progressive education is that it 'makes men think.' Even if banal, such a claim is unexceptionable—provided that there is some attention given to the meaning of the phrase. It will be remembered that, for Dewey, thinking is not something self-contained and aloof. It is a method rather than a thing and cannot easily be divorced from the situation in which it functions. As he wrote in *How We Think*:

> . . . thinking is not a separate process; it is an affair of the *way* in which the vast multitude of objects that are observed and suggested are employed, the way they run together and are *made* to run together, the way they are handled. Consequently any subject, topic, question, is intellectual not *per se* but because of the part it is made to play in directing thought in the life of any particular person. (quoted in 20: 617–18; italics his)

There is indeed a common attitude at the root of all thinking—that of seeking to solve a genuine problem—but there is no monolithic Thinking that is alone the proper subject of education. Intelligence is something to be analyzed and identified as it works; it is not simply the subject of commendation.

But this is not to say that thinking cannot also be an art as well as a tool, nor is it to deny that education can cultivate such an art. In his early *Interest and Effort in Education,* Dewey pointed out that

> at first the interest in the achievement of the end predominates;

> but in the degree in which this interest is bound up with *thoughtful* effort, interest in the end or effect is of necessity transferred to the interest in the means—the causes—which bring it about... It is comparatively a simple matter to secure a transfer of interest from the practical side to experimentation for the sake of discovery. When anyone becomes interested in a problem and in inquiry and learning for the sake of solving the problem, interest is distinctively intellectual... Instead of thinking things out and discovering them for the sake of the successful achievement of an activity, we institute the activity for the sake of finding out something. Then the distinctively intellectual, or theoretical, interest shows itself.*

Encouragement of such intellectual interest must be one of the prime purposes of genuine education, since the experience of the individual is thereby enriched and freed. There is, in the words of John Erskine, a moral obligation to be intelligent.

But experience is, figuratively, vertical as well as horizontal. Transactions are in time as well as in space. This longitudinal dimension, providing another axis for a complete experience, Dewey calls 'continuity.'

Just as experience is not a spatial intruder or somehow unreal, so one period of experience is no more real than another. The live creature at any stage, Dewey points out, is alive at this time and not at another time. It follows that one period of experience is not to be regarded as merely a preparation or education for another period. This repudia-

* The substance of this book goes back to 1896, in Dewey's *Interest as Related to Will (Second Supplement to the Herbart Year Book for 1895;* Bloomington, Ill.), which was reworked in 1913 as *Interest and Effort in Education* (Boston, Houghton Mifflin). The quotation above is found on pp. 83–4, 82.

tion of education-as-preparation provides, of course, the thread which ties Dewey to the other celebrated revolutionaries in education—Rousseau, Herbart, Froebel, Pestalozzi—despite the many fundamental differences between them. It is not, however, any romantic worship of the child which directs Dewey's attack on education-as-preparation. The real difficulty with that approach is its violation of the continuity of experience and therefore of growth. It may be recalled that in the discussion of Dewey's ethics the idea of growth was introduced as illustrative of the fusion of ends and means. The same thought applies here. Growth in education, as in life itself, cannot be a means to any ultimate end except more growth. It is no objection to say that some particular kind of growth or of education is morally preferable to another as an end; that objection would be a misconception of the argument. The growth being understood here is assumed to be full and balanced. It is partial and distorted growth alone that must be rejected. Growth signifies growth in general, a continuum of growth. Indeed, it is this direction of change in the richness and quality of experience which constitutes, for Dewey, the chief moral end-in-view.

> . . . The educative process is all one with the moral process, since the latter is a continuous passage of experience from worse to better. Education has been traditionally thought of as preparation: as learning, acquiring certain things because they will later be useful. The end is remote, and education is getting ready, is a preliminary to something more important to happen later on . . . These ideas contravene the conception that growing, or the continuous reconstruction of experience, is the only end. If at whatever period we choose to take a person, he is still in process of growth, then education is not, save as a by-product,

a preparation for something coming later. Getting from the present the degree and kind of growth there is in it is education. This is a constant function, independent of age. (5: 183–5)*

This interpretation of education as growth, as enrichment of experience, would imply that all persons at all ages are educable, although perhaps not educable in exactly the same way, for each individual has different capacities. If education is the development of one's capacities, it must go far beyond the acquiring of intellectual graces, and it certainly is not confined to formal training or the school. Each individual—such is the present implication—must be given full opportunity to exploit himself and his environment so that he actually does grow. If not, there is a break in the organic continuity of experience. Indeed, were men regarded as fundamentally uneducable, then organic discontinuity should be our basic assumption.

The opportunities for growth will not always be found just lying around. A passive, laissez-faire attitude on the part of society toward the possibilities that alone can bring about all-over growth is dangerously shortsighted. The stimuli to human development have to be actively and deliberately provided. This means more than universal literacy, even at the high school level. There needs to be

* There are, to be sure, other reasons for not accepting the doctrine of education-as-preparation. In *Experience and Education* Dewey argues that 'perhaps the greatest of all pedagogical fallacies is the notion that a person learns only the particular thing he is studying at the time. Collateral learning in the way of formation of enduring attitudes, of likes and dislikes, may be and often is much more important . . . For these attitudes are fundamentally what count in the future. The most important attitude that can be formed is that of desire to go on learning. If impetus in this direction is weakened instead of being intensified, something much more than mere lack of preparation takes place.' (15:49–50)

development, among other directions, along the lines of 'adult education,' a phrase which conceals in a casual and elliptical way the most electric of qualities.* There is power in the idea that the educability of the adult is limited only by his capacities and the available resources. Among his biological and social needs are the satisfaction of curiosity, the sense of accomplishment, the feel of creativeness, the desire for self-expression—in a word, the entire expansion of consciousness. So often these wants are now deflected into bizarre and stultifying vulgarities. Not by leisure but by the use of leisure can men grow. Therefore, education for the citizen must aim to enrich the free time technology is now providing. This is not to be interpreted as regimentation or discipline or some first devious step to cultural totalitarianism. What is intended here is that men need the chance to employ their free time creatively and fruitfully and not be turned over by default to the tender mercies of comic strips and pulp fiction, soap operas, gigantic orgies of professionalized sports and entertainment, all presided over by the advertising impresarios. Instead, encouragement of artistic talents, appreciation of great music and literature, introduction of the fascinations of science and philosophy, cultivation of hobbies, training in the handicrafts—these are but a sample of the paths possible and already being traversed by the more enlightened labor unions, municipal adult-education centers, community colleges, university extension services; indeed there is the suggestion here of a

* These pages are adapted from George R. Geiger's chapter, 'An Experimentalist Approach to Education,' in *Modern Philosophies and Education,* 54th Yearbook of the National Society for the Study of Education, University of Chicago Press, Chicago, 1955. (The adaptation is made with the permission of the secretary of the Society.)

possible folk-school movement. Whether government at the national level in this country will be allowed to contribute to this kind of development is a moot question. It may be remembered that the depression of the 1930s saw the experiment of various government-sponsored art projects, including the beginnings of a federal theatre. It was a tragedy of no small dimension that this whole idea was finally abandoned, not simply because it was allegedly a frill but because, in some peculiar way, it seemed a menace to the American way of life.

These, then, are some of the possible educational outcomes of the concept of experience basic to Dewey's philosophy.

Other aspects of Dewey's philosophy also have significant educational implications, although only one additional example can be developed here. Take the hypothesis that mind is acquired and is not an original bestowal upon the child. If this is so, then it is in the field of education that human nature is literally made as well as changed. (This would be the case whatever definition of education we used, whether the broadest one, in which it refers to nothing less than the changes made in human beings by their experience, or the more limited and usual denotation—deliberate change in the experience and conduct of persons, chiefly but not necessarily young persons, engineered by an organized and self-conscious group.) 'We repeat over and over that man is a social animal,' says Dewey, 'and then confine the significance of this statement to the sphere in which sociality usually seems least evident, politics. The heart of the sociality of man is in education.' (5:185)

This social framework of education is, of course, why the

title of Dewey's most influential book is *Democracy and Education,* and why there is the closest of connections between his political liberalism and his educational progressivism. Take, for example, the suggestion made at the close of the preceding chapter to the effect that democracy requires free communication among its members and the unimpeded sharing of experience. As Dewey puts it:

> The two points selected by which to measure the worth of a form of social life are the extent in which the interests of a group are shared by all its members, and the fullness and freedom with which it interacts with other groups. An undesirable society, in other words, is one which internally and externally sets up barriers to free intercourse and communication of experience. (3:115)

Written during World War I and so only anticipating the national and international 'curtains' of the future, these words show clearly Dewey's constant effort to pull together not only democracy and education, but also the individual and the group, knowledge and communication, experience and participation.

It is this broadening of the range of education which needs to be kept in mind if we turn briefly to still another category, that of liberal education, especially at the college level. Here is a topic that has come in for an almost extravagant amount of attention in recent years. Indeed, the definition of liberal education is itself the issue, for if the 'liberated' individual is the aim of liberal (liberating) education, what is he free from and what is he free for? That he be free of the closed mind, of the intolerance of ignorance, and of the dominance of the specious present would seem obvious to the point of banality. Equally unexceptionable as liberating forces would be the cultivation of critical thought, development of sensitiveness of perception and of creative ability, awareness of cultural history, development of inner resources, understanding of the democratic ethos. But that the liberated man be free to change present society because he can observe it critically and from a historical perspective, change it in the direction of providing those conditions without which an individual cannot grow and enrich his experience—this may seem irrelevant to the purist and subversive to the conservative. Yet an experimental approach, such as Dewey's, would have to settle for some such interpretation of the rôle of liberal education in our culture. For if change, educability, and growth are the basic concepts in all education, then that area called 'liberal'—indeed, *especially* that area called 'liberal'—cannot be set off on some island alone.

Nor can liberal education be simply content with efforts to preserve the past, as is being proposed in some quarters. It must take the lead in understanding, criticizing, and directing cultural change. That knowledge of the past contributes mightily to an understanding of the present is commonplace, and the present interpretation takes full account of it. But that the past be cultivated for its own sake is something else again. It is present and future culture, not past, which is our problem. In the words of Whitehead, 'the only use of a knowledge of the past is to equip us for the present. No more deadly harm can be done to young minds than by depreciation of the present. The present contains all that there is. It is holy ground, for it is the past and it is the future.'*

* *The Organization of Thought, Educational and Scientific,* Lippincott, Philadelphia, 1917, pp. 6–7.

This does not signify that other views of liberal education are unconcerned with present-day problems. But it would appear that the specter of discontinuity haunts the traditionalist here as elsewhere. Apparently he would prepare the adolescent by steeping him in historical materials of classic dimensions, and in the grand style, and then turn him loose, as an adult, on modern problems. Dewey would reverse the emphasis and use contemporary issues that demand drawing on the thought and experience of the past, hoping thereby to maintain historical and logical continuity as well as to enrich the discussion of contemporary issues, which too often are met in over-simple terms and with inappropriate illustrations. It must be remembered that it was their own 'contemporary issues' which produced the Great Books, which, we are advised by some authorities, constitute the core of liberal education; and it is concentration on needed change in the world which will now produce more great books.

The directing of liberal education toward the solution of contemporary problems—to the end that men can live richly and humanly—can be regarded as limited or illiberal only if those problems are misunderstood and undervalued. 'Contemporary problems' include nothing less than war and peace, extinction or survival; they also include the extension of a democratic ethic; the place of scientific intelligence in solving problems, including value problems; the development of esthetic appreciation as far as man's capacities will allow; the scrutiny of economic and political institutions—the horizons are unlimited. These are not 'social problems' in some parochial sense. They are comprehensive enough to include even an appreciation of the humanities! But to circumscribe liberal education by refusing it any other office than that of considering the place of the classics is a crippling limitation. It would tend toward the cultivation of 'gentlemen' in a very obnoxious sense.

To hold that concern with the present is illiberal is of a piece with the idea that 'vocational' education presents the grand antithesis to liberal education. Here is the illiberal bogey always available for drubbing. Now, it is very easy—and very correct—to sneer at the vocationalizing of much of modern education. But lofty contempt for practical subjects is not necessarily the hallmark of the scholar, even when the examples chosen are calculated to get a laugh—pie making, camp leadership, window cleaning, pre-pharmacy, salesmanship. For these, and other egregious examples, no one is prepared to be apologetic. But to assume that training for making a living has no place whatsoever in liberal education is to assume that education has no context. It is to make the pleasantly superior assumption that college is a place to spend four happy years immaculately preserved from contamination with the outside, a sort of unruptured chrysalis in which ivy can be enjoyed, green lawns trod, and precious books read, a refuge and vacation from a naughty world. It is also to assume that preparation for law school, for selling bonds, for private preparatory-school teaching, for corporation management, or for working on Madison Avenue is somehow *not* vocational. Veblen could find no better example of invidious comparison than this!

Genuine vocational education goes far beyond the caricaturish limitations imposed on it by the educational elite and by the genteel tradition. From an individual's earliest years through the latest ones to be served by an expanding program of continuing education, there can be a 'vocational' approach which will exploit every possible device for making men think, for making them sensitive to the authentic and imperative problems of their own careers, for enriching the making of a living so that it becomes more than a casually neglected instrument. This enlargement will unquestionably employ the resources of liberal education, even the purest—but they will be fitted into a situation and will not be expected to supply a possibly factitious one.

For the last few pages we have been concerned with educational problems extending beyond what ordinarily comes under the rubric 'progressive'—although the restriction of this word to the education of children, especially of very young children, seems a serious limitation of the sweep of Dewey's philosophy of experience. If we return now to the more usual connotations of progressive or the newer education, an almost inevitable equivocation emerges or, more appropriately, a determination to have one's cake and eat it too. On the one hand, it is undoubtedly the case that during the first generation of the present century, yet extending further back than that, the school has been reconstructed in a dramatic way, and not only in this country. There have been revolutionary changes, and whether they are regarded as a cultural liability or asset there is no question but that they are part of a formidable movement to which the name of John Dewey has been attached. On the other hand, this revolution in education, like so many other revolutions, has been seriously deflected and never had a chance to develop fully. Criticisms are generally based on the untenable assumption that the newer education has been fully realized and universally dominant, and that what we have today, including much that is indefensible, is a direct result of that dominance. But progressive education has had to fight a powerful counter-revolution at every point of its advance—a counter-revolution which constantly increased its strength as the century moved into an age of anxiety and of nerve failure—while at the same time it had to reckon with the extravagances of certain extremists; it has never made much of an impact beyond the elementary school and has certainly never thoroughly permeated the public school system; and it has been unable to get across the special import of scientific thinking, which Dewey has regarded as the very core of educational reform and which is so clearly an outcome of his principal philosophic premise.* 'If the method of science,' he writes, 'had ever been consistently and continuously applied throughout the day-by-day work of the school in all subjects, I should be more impressed by this . . . appeal than I am'—the appeal, namely, to the inadequacy of science to handle most human problems. (15:108)

As we have had occasion to remark before, present-day suspicion of science, when it is honest, is based on the belief that scientific method has been on the ascendancy for lo these many years, and look at the results! This is as superficial as is fashion itself. To assume that we have been living in an era consistently dominated by the employment of scientific method in all fields of human problem solving—including the fields of the person, of society, and of values—is so bizarre that the mere statement of it will stand as a refutation. Similarly, to assume that an education devoted

* For a good recent summary of the American school at mid-century a recommended book is that of I. L. Kandel, *American Education in the Twentieth Century*, Harvard University Press, Cambridge, 1957.

to the cultivation of individuality and to the true enrichment of the ongoing experience of every man, and dedicated, among other things, to the intrinsic worth of the child rather than to the child as a step to something else, and orientated to the naturalistic and scientific explanation of human difficulties—to assume that this kind of education has taken over the American school, and for a sufficient period of time to be judged, is sheer fantasy.

There is nothing of apology in this argument. For even if so-called progressive education has been clipped, strained, and twisted, the results it has been able to achieve in the twentieth century have been so pervasive that even in the traditional, and occasionally in the religious, school they have become commonplaces. It must be repeated that the newer education did not spring fully armed from the head of Dewey or anyone else. In addition to an educational movement reaching back some centuries, there was the experimental background of the developmental psychologists at the end of the nineteenth and the beginning of the twentieth centuries, and of psychoanalysis itself. The importance of the individual child was becoming established. Yet because the American school and also the American family have been changed and the child treated quite differently from what had been the case before the 'Dewey School' at the University of Chicago began its pioneering work, it does not follow that we can now forget the presupposition that the child still needs individual attention. Nor, to go to the other extreme, does it mean that the 'liberation' of the five-year-old can still serve as a clarion battlecry, much less that such liberation implies absence of discipline and rigor. Dewey has argued persistently that a loose and sentimental idea of freedom is as dangerous as authoritarianism. Certain new and appropriate ways of handling the child, in the school and in the home, have been built into our culture as a result of an educational and psychological revolution, and certain excesses have unquestionably accompanied them, but to remedy the latter does not mean we must scrap what already has been achieved.

Dewey's general reputation, here and abroad, will undoubtedly vary with the degree to which the newer education becomes a stable and recognized element of any culture, since in no other field has his influence been so dominant. This specialized dominance is of mixed value. The reason why it is mixed is that Dewey's reputation becomes a kind of hostage for what has passed for the newer education, an education that has not always made clear its theoretical formulations and has even tended to deprecate them. Along the same line, it must be recognized that the profession of teacher-education has, at times, become overspecialized and narrow, with the result that 'philosophy of education' has occasionally been put aside as not really essential or has been distorted into a rationalization and an apologetic. No such problem exists in Dewey's own work, where a general theory of experience provides the basis for particular applications, as in politics and education, and where, in turn, the theory is itself open to examination for its consistency and human relevance.

More than a man's reputation is at stake, however, when an unnatural separation develops between philosophy and education, whether the separation originates because of the aloofness of the academician or the haste of the specialist. The population explosion about to hit the schools has made the American public aware, as never before, of at least the physical and personnel inadequacies of the country's educational resources. It may not be too much to hope that the theoretical inadequacies may also become apparent. These are not inadequacies in the sense that theories of education are not available. Any textbook in philosophy of education will give the spread from authoritarianism to laissez-faire and all the subtle variations in between. The inadequacy lies in the gap between an almost universal acceptance of a democratic ethic, unbuttoned as it may be, and a hesitation, becoming occasionally almost paralytic, to think about the educational demands made by that acceptance. Unless that gap is closed, and quickly, there may be a fall-out far worse than the original explosion.

To close that gap questions like these need to be attended to: What kind of education do American citizens expect for the millions of children now flooding the schools? These millions are indeed educable, but in what way? What philosophical and political presuppositions—however general and informal they may be—are at the base of the new educational demands? And what effects, short-range and long-range, may be expected to follow? The integration between an enriched experience, a liberated intelligence, and an experimental education, such as that envisaged by John Dewey, may or not prove to be theoretically adequate. But to put it aside as somehow 'old-fashioned and irrelevant' (I quote) would be to court disaster.

10. Scientific Humanism

To have introduced words like 'old-fashioned' and 'irrelevant' into a discussion of Dewey, even when quoting accurately, may seem to be gratuitous or unnecessarily defensive. But the tendency to by-pass Dewey needs constantly to be reckoned with, for it has become a characteristic one and is far more slippery than the forthright attacks which used to greet his ideas. Even the neutral college student, for example, is now inclined to class Dewey with Emerson and Whitman as representing certain classic American virtues which are rather out of style and which are no longer revolutionary. They may even be conservative!

It is more than the fact that Dewey was born a century ago that accounts for his seeming dated. As has been said, there is little agonizing about the soul in his writings; there is no acceptance of knowledge, particularly knowledge of values, that transcends rational and scientific methods; there is no trace of supernaturalism; and there is perhaps too little linguistic analysis. These are the things, among others, that contemporary philosophers are talking about. Like the philosophers, if for different reasons, the general public has also turned to other fashions. Among these of course is 'the return to religion.' It will be important to discover what Dewey proposes in the field of religion not only because of the intrinsic claims of the subject but also to see if the position he represents can develop its own special claim upon us.

The abiding and canonical theme of religion is clearly that of the supernatural, of the world which lies beyond experience. Indeed the two seem almost synonymous. It is notable that Dewey attempts, especially in *A Common Faith*, to show that there is no necessary connection between religion and the supernatural and to clear the ground for a humanistic and naturalistic religion. First, he distinguishes between 'religion' and 'religious'. The former as a noun denotes a thing, such as an institution, a body of doctrine, or at least a set of beliefs; furthermore, the substantive character of the institution, doctrine, or beliefs generally involves 'recognition on the part of man of some unseen higher power as having control of his destiny and as being entitled to obedience, reverence, and worship.' Religious, for Dewey, connotes quality of an experience, consummatory quality such as that found in esthetic experience; similarly it is not circumscribed by any special content, like the gods in this case. It is a reaction or attitude which may be evoked by many objects.

Many of these objects, however, have been encumbered by accretions, coming from a time in history when, as it were, supernaturalistic explanations of human problems and achievements were appropriate and even 'natural,' since there were no others. Reverence then for the unseen higher powers that alone had control of man's destiny was fitting. The religious quality developed accordingly. But the path of this development became one-way, walled in as it was by tradition. Dewey proposes that at least in imagination we start afresh and ask what might be expected if man's religious experiences were allowed to find outlet in forms more congenial to scientific and rational and artistic understanding. After all, man has already used imaginative selection within the area of the supernatural, coming to believe in 'a wise and loving spirit rather than in madcap ghosts or sheer force,' and having made this choice he has, Dewey notes, 'entered upon a road that has not yet come to an end. We have reached a point that invites us to proceed farther.' (12:7)

On this point Dewey has been misunderstood not merely by the devout but even by naturalists like Bertrand Russell and George Santayana. He has been accused of 'cosmic impiety,' of exaggerating the importance of the human factor (foreground) at the expense of the rest of nature (background). Unless that background comes more into the picture, they aver, the whole perspective is distorted, humanism runs rampant, and because of this aggrandizement of the ego almost anything can happen—and has happened. We need therefore to quote Dewey at some length, because the misunderstanding here is serious and unnecessary. The following words are from *A Common Faith,* but the same point can be found in *Experience and Nature, Art as Experience,* and in earlier works:

> The essentially unreligious attitude is that which attributes human achievement and purpose to man in isolation from the world of physical nature and his fellows. Our successes are dependent upon the co-operation of nature . . . Natural piety . . . may rest upon a just sense of nature as the whole of which we are parts, while it also recognizes that we are parts that are marked by intelligence and purpose, having the capacity to strive by their aid to bring conditions into greater consonance with what is humanly desirable. (12:25)

> . . . Aggressive atheism seems to me to have something in common with traditional supernaturalism . . . What I have in mind is the exclusive preoccupation of both militant atheism

and supernaturalism with man in isolation . . . Militant atheism is also affected by a lack of natural piety. The ties binding man to nature that poets have always celebrated are passed over lightly. The attitude taken is often that of man living in an indifferent and hostile world and issuing blasts of defiance. A religious attitude, however, needs the sense of a connection of man, in the way of both dependence and support, with the enveloping world that the imagination feels is a universe . . . A humanistic religion, if it excludes our relation to nature, is pale and thin, as it is presumptuous, when it takes humanity as an object of worship. (12: 52–4.)

These words should be clear enough not only to clear Dewey from any possible charge of cosmic impiety, but also, turning about, to expose something like Russell's 'free man' and his worship, which almost implies the non-naturalistic position that man must defy a seemingly hostile universe before he does anything else.

When, however, we come to exactly what Dewey intends by the religious attitude, certain difficulties will be encountered. He writes that 'any activity pursued in behalf of an ideal end against obstacles and in spite of threats of personal loss because of conviction of its general and enduring value is religious in quality' and that "whatever introduces genuine perspective is religious.' (12: 27, 24.) In other words, whatever we believe in seriously, whatever enlists our basic value commitments, what we feel is genuinely worth living for—these will arouse an experience fittingly called religious. Certainly this interpretation is generous enough to enlarge the idea of 'religious' far beyond the historical limits of the supernatural, but the result would seem to thin out its meaning until a religious experience becomes indistinguishable from any other significant experience, or so to expand it, on the other hand, that nothing would escape its touch. Consequently, almost no one could really be said to be irreligious, since there is surely something everyone takes seriously. The communist and the fascist, the fanatic and the crank, in token of their pursuit of an ideal against obstacles and in spite of threats of personal loss would be religious men, because of conviction. The word 'religious' *is* used in this sense—and was so used long before Dewey—but only at the sacrifice of any possible ethical judgment. Similarly we may recognize that men like what they like and thereby enjoy a valid experience without accepting this as an esthetic judgment about the fine arts. We are concerned here with the absence of an explicit moral criterion in Dewey's definition.

However, in his discussion of ideals as part of, rather than as outside, nature, Dewey does introduce a moral dimension into the religious experience. As might be expected, it is determined by the richness and fullness of the experience and the rational resolution of difficulties; these of course have provided the basis for his theories of value, education, and intelligence. In his own words:

> There exist concretely and experimentally goods—the values of art in all its forms, of knowledge, of effort and of rest after striving, of education and fellowship, of friendship and love, or growth in mind and body . . . There are values, goods, actually realized upon a natural basis—the goods of human association, of art and knowledge. The idealizing imagination seizes upon the most precious things found in the climacteric moments of experience and projects them. We need no external criterion and guarantee of their goodness. They are had, they exist as good, and out of them we frame our ideal ends. (12: 51, 48.)

These words may provide one last occasion to confront what sometimes looks like a major difficulty in Dewey's ethics. It is the joint assertion of the position that, as in the above, goods are simply had and need no guarantee for their goodness except perhaps 'the climacteric moments of experience,' and of the equally characteristic position that goods rest upon critical thought and the intelligent solving of problems. The burden of an earlier discussion* was to come to terms with this double-aspect approach, as of course Dewey has done many times, and to show that the distinction between the non-cognitive and the cognitive, between 'having' and 'knowing,' is a valid distinction and no paradox. There are indeed goods which need no ulterior justification, just as there are endings and closures in nature itself. Consummated experience is a natural immediate happening, precious in its own right and not susceptible to any form of theorizing, least of all moral. It is in this realm of direct havings that Dewey finds the natural basis for moral ideals, and it is to this realm that he makes his sometimes poetic apostrophes. But there are also indirect goods or values. Without repeating what was said before on this matter, we can simply point out that problems will arise among the natural immediacies—conflicts will emerge, decisions must be made and intelligent decision thereby given its opportunity, and a realm of value appears in which conflicts are mediated. Immediate goods become reflective goods, the holiday world of esthetics turns into the workaday world of ethics; but when the times are happy, the workaday world will have its sustained incandescent moments; and thoughtful experience, like art, will take on the quality of consummation. This merger of the immediate

* See Chapter II, p. 21 ff., and Chapter III p. 42 ff.

and the reflective provides, I take it, the basis of the religious experience, and it also provides Dewey with a standard of judgment: it establishes that 'genuine perspective' which alone is worthy of being regarded as religious.

Such a 'unity of all ideal ends arousing us to desire and action' is also worthy of being called 'God.' Dewey here introduces, albeit with a good bit of hesitation, this highly confusing term—confusing certainly for a naturalist—and it must be acknowledged that his use of it is more than a little infelicitous. The way he intends to use 'God' is found in the following lines:

> Suppose for the moment that the word 'God' means the ideal ends that at a given time and place one acknowledges as having authority over his volition and emotion, the values to which one is supremely devoted, as far as these ends, through imagination, take on unity . . . This idea of God, or of the divine, is also connected with all the natural forces and conditions—including man and human association—that promote the growth of the ideal and that further its realization . . . A religious attitude . . . needs the sense of a connection of man, in the way of both dependence and support, with the enveloping world that the imagination feels is a universe. Use of the words 'God' or 'divine' to convey the union of actual with ideal may protect man from a sense of isolation and from consequent despair or defiance. (12: 42, 50, 53)

These words serve to repudiate once more the superficial charge of cosmic impiety, but whether theistic language needs to be employed in that service and as a symbol for the unity of the ideal and the actual is surely debatable.

In any case, use of 'God' furnishes no beginning compromise with supernaturalism. Dewey's chief argument throughout is an attempt to counter what, early and late, have been some of the reasons given for reliance on the unseen higher powers which control man's destiny. For example, human ignorance about the grand questions of the universe and the soul has characteristically prepared the way for an excursion to what is purportedly beyond natural explanation. In modern days this turning to an extra-nature has taken a Platonic form in which 'wisdom' is to be distinguished from 'science,' the former appropriate for the province of values and the humanities, the latter for facts and the practical arts, the one dealing with ends, the other with means. It is then easy to step from something like wisdom, which is above science, to a special kind of knowledge, quite beyond the ordinary precincts of nature. Dewey refuses to accept present or past ignorance as a reason for imputing a necessary opaqueness to any aspect of experience. It would be bold to the point of rashness, he insists, to maintain that (as an illustration) intimate personal experience, with its value-laden moments, 'will never come under the ken of natural knowledge.' To maintain that it will not and to introduce at the same time a dimension beyond ordinary knowledge is to beg the question in a most egregious way. The question begged is not whether there are any non-cognitive experiences—that there are is constantly affirmed by Dewey—but whether there is any substitute for *knowledge,* for the reflective method of solving problems. Such a method is called 'scientific' when certain rigorous canons have been observed, and its applicability depends on whether the experience involved is a matter of inquiry or one of immediate enjoyment. It does not depend on an a priori determination to restrict science to mere instrumentalities and so to downgrade it, as Dewey puts it, in favor of 'belief so fixed in advance that it can never be modified.'

The dominance of method, distinguishing here between the natural, where beliefs are arrived at and modified by tested inquiry, and the non-natural, where already established beliefs are held to be unmodifiable by such inquiry, is of course the major emphasis in Dewey's philosophy. The all-important problem, writes Joseph Ratner, is the problem of method, to which he adds: 'There is nothing inherent in the nature of things that makes it possible for the method of experimentation—or of controlled inquiry—to be employed in certain fields and nowhere else.' * It should be superfluous to repeat what was argued earlier, that this experimental method is not dependent upon any particular body of subject-matter, e.g. the physical sciences, or upon any particular laboratory routine, such as that of analytical or mechanical models; and that therefore it does not rise or fall with the prominence accorded to special techniques from time to time. Dewey feels for this reason that anti-naturalists are mistaken when they interpret a turning away from the classic theory of mechanicalism to an organismic and synthetic approach in, say, the life sciences as also a turning away from naturalism and thus a step in the direction of something beyond intelligent scrutiny. On the contrary:

> . . . the change in the modern scientific view of nature simply brings man and nature nearer together. We are no longer compelled to choose between explaining away what is distinctive

* From the concluding page of his introduction to Dewey's philosophy in *Intelligence in the Modern World.*

in man through reducing him to another form of a mechanical model and the doctrine that something literally supernatural marks him off from nature. The less mechanical—in its older sense—physical nature is found to be, the closer is man to nature. (12: 55.)

The disposition in contemporary science to talk of organic process and change rather than of fixed mechanisms is not a repudiation of naturalistic explanation, and if, as Peter Drucker and others have been saying, a 'new' philosophy needs to accompany this disposition, it, too, must avoid mistaking a change in explanatory categories for surrender of an entire position.

But is naturalistic explanation capable of arousing a religious emotion? Can man indeed develop a 'devotion, so intense as to be religious, to intelligence as a force in social action'? This is a crucial question for any humanist, and one that needs to be looked at rather carefully.

First, there is the matter of words like 'humanism' and 'naturalism' themselves. Each has, in its history, been used to express so many things that it requires qualifying phrases and clauses or other symbolic devices necessary for detecting precise referents. For example, 'humanism' can mean anything from the rather precious school of literary criticism which has flourished in this country to a generous and systematic philosophy interested in man and his works. In between these limits could be identified: the Renaissance delight in the rediscovery of pagan classics, an emancipated religious movement of modern days, a British synonym for pragmatism, a theory of liberal arts education—and the list would be far from complete. The same is true of 'naturalism.' Excluding its uses in the realms of literary criticism and the life sciences, philosophical dictionaries can still note twenty to thirty different meanings which have become attached to the word, with the spectrum extending from a crude materialism to a sensitive awareness of the continuities underlying man's relations to the world. What is important for the present discussion is to discover how these two words, along with 'scientific,' can be used together and just what they may have in common. This will provide us not only with usable meanings but possibly with a summary of Dewey's philosophy.

We may begin with the assumption that values are man-made and man-directed: they are not intimations of a transcendent realm of goods. But this humanistic assumption is also a naturalistic one, for we can then postulate the continuity of man with the rest of nature and reject any discontinuity between nature and what allegedly lies beyond it. Further, the continuity is, at least in part, methodological, which is to say that a human tool, scientific method, is what does or can provide the integration drawing together man and his values and the non-human world. In addition to this cluster of premises, there should be included the presuppositions that nature and experience are not antithetical and that, since predictions can be made which are subject to verification or disverification, the world can be known and controlled to a degree sufficient to be significant. These are commonplaces in science. To insist that they should also be commonplaces for philosophy would be another step toward identifying the character of scientific humanism. Add to these the acceptance of the genuine uncertainties and incommensurabilities in that experience as well as its neat and logical order; for there are discontinuities and gaps (such as those recognized by physics itself), inconsistencies and frustrations, evils for which no remedies have been discovered, disappointments and setbacks, whole areas of whirling and pluralistic confusion. Comfortable as it would be to do so, the humanist and naturalist cannot honestly manufacture a universe or even a culture which is altogether smooth, sure, and sanitary.

In returning now to the question whether an attitude represented by such a constellation of premises is religiously available, it can be suggested first that there is literally nothing that cannot evoke a religious experience. A significant section of anthropology is devoted to the items of human worship; the range is almost unlimited and occasionally unspeakable. There is no antecedent reason why something like scientific intelligence and a naturalistic spirit should be—at least as Dewey uses the word—religiously unavailable. But this, of course, is much too negative a way of putting it. The question is rather, cannot emotional commitment be made to, as Charles Morris has called it, the Promethean way of life? In Prometheus seizing fire from the gods we have the picture of a Maker, a technologist, a transformer. We have the symbol of continuous and responsible reconstruction of man's world. We have at the same time the sign for sacrifice and risk, since Prometheus was bound. Here is a view of man and of nature which offers a challenge as searching as any that human genius has ever called forth. It offers a promise, too, since Prometheus was finally unbound.

The challenge is not simply that the world and the human spirit be changed; it is rather that scientific humanism presents the tool and the process to make that reconstruction possible. Intelligent inquiry institutionalizes change; the very operation of scientific method and of critical thinking alters the situation. Thus, while a humanistic philosophy carries the moral responsibility to re-form the world, it carries also, as an intrinsic part of its methodology, the implementation without which moral responsibility becomes frustrating. Emotional commitment would seem to be an integral part of scientific humanism because means are provided as well as ends. Yet this is too theoretical a way of expressing it. The history of a great section of Western culture has already demonstrated the emotional fire and revolutionary power of man's faith in man; his commitments *have* been detonated. Not simply the history of man's conquest of physical nature, but the record of his principal victories over political and economic oppression have been written in terms of confidence in natural means. The argument that humanism has failed to make an impression on men is limited too narrowly to the fields of classic religion and creed.

To be sure, this may be what the anti-naturalist is waiting for us to say. Yet one does not have to be an anti-naturalist to read the daily papers or to see that the secular triumphs of humanism have brought no comparable moral victories. Perhaps the contrary. One would need to be a rather smug optimist not to admit the vulnerability of naturalism on this score. But it must be recalled that we are here estimating the emotional and 'religious' appeal of scientific humanism, and for such an appeal an admitted vulnerability is not necessarily a handicap. Certainly man has not solved his great problems; in many areas he has made barely a start, if that. But to assume, as the contemporary anti-naturalist does, that something like scientific humanism has already had a long record of failure and must now be supplanted by something else is to misread history disastrously and perhaps dishonestly. It would be to assume that the tools of naturalism and intelligence have been man's consistent and longtime tools. But the spirit of scientific humanism is clearly a product of the Scientific Revolution. Actually it is even later, for the new sciences gave their first consideration to conquering physical nature rather than to saving man from himself. This may or may not be a criticism of the scientific enterprise: it is an indication of its youth. The struggle to turn the methods of science to the problems of man is just beginning; to give up that struggle at this point would be surrender of the most desperate and indefensible sort. And unless youth, adventure, and prospect are indeed dead—which they certainly are not—such surrender can hardly prove inspiring.

On the contrary, if any blame for modern moral defeatism is to be portioned out, if responsibility is to be fixed for man's inhumanity to man, supernaturalism must be held as guilty as anything else. Certainly it has had a longer period to demonstrate its supposed competence and to practice its exorcisms and exhortations. For it to accuse a scientific naturalism that is barely getting under way for not yet having made man a god is impertinence of a peculiarly arrogant kind. In any event, religious motivation cannot meaningfully be confined to what may well be stale and ancient complaints. The electricity of faith will illuminate a secular religion such as that of Prometheus because of the very hazards of its promise, because of adventure. It is not an overbearing religion. It does look to the future and it is completely unconvinced that man and his intelligence have been tried and found wanting; but it is necessarily promissory and therefore, to a degree, on the defensive. Its trust in human resources is neither blasé nor naïve. Man has accomplished this much: he can accomplish more. Whether he will or not is a matter of hope and hard work. But surely he will not accomplish more if he surrenders, turning to wishful rationalizations about a supernatural world and a superhuman instrument.

Were the Deweyan naturalism being recommended here of the 'old-fashioned' kind—that of reductionism and 'nothing but'—its claims upon us would still be emotionally arid. But it must be pointed out once more that the inability of natural science to discover in the non-human world anything that directly resembles value or purpose is no reason for despair. One does not have to gird up one's loins heroically, like Bertrand Russell's free man, in order to worship 'the love and achievement and noonday brightness' which are supposedly alien to atoms and their accidental collocations. A non-humanistic, and therefore a dated, naturalism which sees no purpose in the world finds it hard to account for purpose in man. But man takes his purposes seriously even if the universe does not—although that is an inaccurate way of putting it. Man is part of the universe, part of nature, and as 'natural' as anything else; his values and his hopes are as empirically real as anything the traditional naturalist could applaud. What is beautiful and lovely is no less so for being human. And it is natural to be human. Modern, humanistic naturalism—usually called scientific humanism—will not fall into the dualistic trap which even Russell's emancipated free man seems to stumble into, the trap severing value from nature. Humanism is pale and thin, to quote Dewey again, only when 'it takes humanity as an object of worship' to the exclusion of 'our relation to nature.' But uniting man with nature and cementing the union with the method of free intelligence can bring a new vision which poets, and even mystics, will learn to celebrate.

Epilogue

Epilogue

A good bit of attention has been paid in the preceding pages to the humanistic and naturalistic spirit—whether it be called 'religious' is a matter of taste. The reason should by now be clear. John Dewey's philosophy will stand or fall to the degree in which this spirit prevails or is obscured. Not that his contribution is confined to a general exposition of naturalism and a commemoration of the worth of man: these interests have been with us in the West at least since the pre-Socratics. His particular contribution has been something more specific—the outline of a method, a method designed to replace the classic end-means dualism with a transactional approach and directed to enlisting the power of science to solve the problems of men. This expression of naturalism will compete for the imaginations of men unless their nerve finally fails.

It may be, as Clarence Ayres has said, that we are indeed approaching the end of a period of compromise; perhaps this is why men's nerves are strained. There has been an uneasy division of the world, a division by which science received jurisdiction over the 'outer' world of things and facts, whereas something else, call it what you will, was to command the 'inside' region of the spirit and of values. This armistice, of course, has been broken. The inside world is no longer exempt from scientific investigation, nor are values themselves. But this initial penetration has been resisted, and it is precisely this resistance which is responsible, at least in part, for the ambiguous reception accorded to science, making it liable, as it were, for the very failures over which it has had no jurisdiction. It is for this reason if nothing else, Dewey holds, that scientific method must extend its domain or risk having its prime discovery, human intelligence, regarded as no more than a kind of amoral gimmick. In his ninetieth year, in a kind of valedictory,* he addressed himself again to the familiar, almost tedious, ambivalence that science provokes today—it can destroy man as well as save him. Recognition of this Janus-quality, however banal it has become, can be an asset but only if appreciation of the undoubted two-facedness of science leads to diagnosis of how it came about and what can be done to turn the faces in the same direction. In one of his last counsels to us Dewey restates his chief point this way:

> A hiatus exists within scientific inquiry, and it is intimately connected with our present disturbed and unsettled state. It is for the philosophers today to encourage and further methods of inquiry into human and moral subjects similar to those their predecessors in their day encouraged and furthered in the physical and physiological sciences: in short to bring into existence a kind of knowledge which, by being thoroughly humane, is entitled to the name *moral*. Its absence seems to explain the prevailing worldwide state of uncertainty, suspense, discontent, and strife. It would also seem to indicate with startling clearness that the one thing of prime importance today is development of methods of scientific inquiry to supply us with the humane or moral knowledge now conspicuously lacking.†

* 'Philosophy's Future in Our Scientific Age,' in *Commentary*, October 1949, pp. 388–94.

† Ibid. p. 391.

Epilogue

The race today, as Irwin Edman has said, is between intelligence and catastrophe. The alternatives to intelligence are 'fanaticism, nihilism, sentimentalism, triviality, or despair.' In less dramatic language Ernest Nagel has made the same point: 'A judicious confidence in the power of reason to ennoble the human estate may seem shallow to an age in which, despite the dominant position in it of scientific technology, there is a growing and pervasive distrust of the operations of free intelligence . . . But the cultivation of [the] intellectual temper is a fundamental condition for every liberal civilization.' *

This is perhaps the note on which to end, although codas are usually extravagant and full of bravura. The quiet note is produced by the position that a liberal civilization takes, lying as it does between the extremes of distrust of human experience at one end and intolerant confidence in dogmatic formulas at the other. And such a liberal civilization is always a matter of hope. Perhaps, then, it is not fair to John Dewey to place his ideas against the crazy background of a fugitive present. We may say instead that when men are finally ready to apply intelligent inquiry to the solving of their problems—and if they never are, nothing more need be said—the thought of John Dewey will be there.

* *Sovereign Reason*, The Free Press, Glencoe, Illinois, 1954, p. 308.

Bibliography

Bibliography

The following is a chronologically arranged list of titles of books by John Dewey quoted most frequently in the text. It is, of course, not a complete bibliography. The most convenient bibliography will be found in the Schilpp volume (see below) pp. 611-76. The number at the left is the key for references quoted.

1. *How We Think*. Boston: D. C. Heath & Co., 1910. (The revised edition, 1933, is the one that will be quoted.)
2. *The Influence of Darwin on Philosophy*. New York: Henry Holt, 1910.
3. *Democracy and Education*. New York: Macmillan, 1916.
4. *Essays in Experimental Logic*. Chicago: University of Chicago Press, 1916. (The reprint of 1953 by Dover Publications will be used here for reference.)
5. *Reconstruction in Philosophy*. New York: Henry Holt, 1920 (reprinted in several other editions).
6. *Human Nature and Conduct*. New York: Henry Holt, 1922.
7. *Experience and Nature*. Chicago: Open Court, 1925. (1929 ed. will be quoted here.)
8. *The Public and Its Problems*. New York: Henry Holt, 1927.
9. *The Quest for Certainty*. New York: Minton, Balch, 1929.
10. *Individualism, Old and New*. New York: Minton, Balch, 1930.
11. *Art as Experience*. New York: Minton, Balch, 1934.
12. *A Common Faith*. New Haven: Yale University Press, 1934.
13. *Liberalism and Social Action*. New York: G. P. Putnam's Sons, 1935.

14. *Logic: The Theory of Inquiry.* New York: Henry Holt, 1938.

15. *Experience and Education.* New York: Macmillan, 1938.

16. *Freedom and Culture.* New York: G. P. Putnam's Sons, 1939.

17. *Problems of Men.* New York: Philosophical Library, 1946.

18. *Knowing and the Known* (with Arthur F. Bentley). Boston: The Beacon Press, 1949.

also:

19. *The Philosophy of John Dewey,* edited by Paul Schilpp, Evanston, Ill.: Northwestern University, 1939.

20. *Intelligence in the Modern World: John Dewey's Philosophy,* edited by Joseph Ratner, New York: The Modern Library, Random House, 1939.

Index

Index

Index

Index

Index

Index